Now Sings My Soul

READERS EDITION

NEW SONGS FOR THE LORD

LINDA BONNEY OLIN

Now Sings My Soul—Readers Edition
New Songs for the Lord

Published by Linda Bonney Olin, New York, USA
www.LindaBonneyOlin.com

ISBN-13: 978-0-9911865-6-3
ISBN-10: 991186567

CONTENTS

PREFACE

Now Sings My Soul: New Songs for the Lord offers more than one hundred original texts. They don't claim to be highbrow works of sacred music or literature. They simply seek a place among the hymns and faith songs people find meaningful and love to sing.

Songs in this collection help our souls sing wherever we may be, right now, on our walk with the Lord. Sometimes we sing for joy; sometimes we mourn our losses and lament our circumstances. We confess our failings; we thank God for our salvation. We sing praises, proclaiming our confidence in God's power and goodness and love. Even when that confidence wavers, we can raise our questions to the Lord in songs as heartfelt as David's psalms.

As we sing, the Lord speaks to *us*, too. He assures us that he is here, and that he loves us dearly. He teaches us his ways and urges us to follow them. He strengthens our spiritual bond with one another. He reminds us of his mighty, compassionate deeds in the past. He opens our minds to what we can become through his grace in the future, here on earth and into eternity.

The imagery, language, and themes in my lyrics may be broadly categorized as Christian, but they don't always explicitly refer to Jesus Christ and New Testament scriptures. Some express faith in the Lord God more generally or reference Old Testament passages. Some simply explore what it means to exist in relationship with the Almighty.

Every faith community will, of course, apply its own doctrinal standards and use its own judgment on acceptable content and style for congregational singing, for a choir or soloist in the worship setting, and for inspirational music programs. For private devotions and personal enjoyment, you are free to decide which songs ring true to your beliefs and experiences and your needs at this moment.

For me, "Father God" is a cherished, intimate way of relating to God, as it was for Jesus. And I acknowledge God as the sovereign ruler of all. Accordingly, my texts do not conform to notions of "inclusive language" that exclude patriarchal imagery and references to God as lord or king. I also choose not to depersonalize God with neuter pronouns or use stilted repetitions of nouns in order to eliminate every masculine pronoun for the deity. Those who wish to emphasize the gender-transcending nature of God are welcome to sing feminine or neutral pronouns instead, provided that doing so does not impair the scriptural, thematic, or poetic integrity of my text.

The theme piece of this collection, "Now Sings My Soul a New Song," leads the lineup. Next come songs associated with the church calendar, beginning with Advent and Christmas. The rest are loosely grouped but follow no formal order. You may notice a few quirks in the numbering. The song texts are numbered to correspond with the score numbers of the musical settings, which appear in other editions.

This Readers Edition and the full edition present the texts in stanza format for easy reading by devotional readers and worship planners. Be forewarned: My verses don't always stick to conventional hymn meters. Some lines may sound awkward when read as poetry. Rest assured, those hiccups will be cured when they're sung to the music they were written for.

The tune for each text is named below the verses. Some of the musical settings are my own compositions. Usually, however, I seek and tweak a public domain hymn tune whose distinctive features complement the phrasing and mood of the text.

The term "alt." next to a tune name will alert you that the tune has been altered from its previously published form. For example, I may have added a pickup note at the beginning of the song. You can hear my version of all the tunes on the Now Sings My Soul~Audio page at the Faith Songs website (LindaBonneyOlin.com).

In my writing process, text and tune intertwine—a sort of marriage made in heaven. I won't go so far as to say, "What Linda has joined together, let no one put asunder," but please keep in mind that sending my texts on blind dates with other tunes may diminish their singability and message power.

To accurately follow the musical settings and fully appreciate the lyrics, I strongly advise singers and musicians to choose either the full edition or the Musicians Edition of this book. Both include complete scores with large, legible font on 8.5" x 11" pages.

Below each song's text is a list of suggested themes and occasions for using the song in worship, plus a selection of scripture verses for study and meditation. Undoubtedly you will find additional relevant verses in the Bible.

Scripture and theme indexes and an alphabetical index of song titles are provided in the back of the book. A few recommended Bible verses that amplify specific phrases but don't deal with a major theme of the overall text have beene omitted from the scripture index.

Resources for using this music will be posted on the Faith Songs website (LindaBonneyOlin.com). You can reach me via the contact form there. Please take a moment to look at my other books and music too, especially Bible studies and dramas that use songs to enhance the story.

May you be as richly blessed in reading and singing these new songs for the Lord as I've been in writing them!

—Linda Bonney Olin

O sing to the Lord a new song;
sing to the Lord, all the earth.

Sing to the Lord, bless his name;
tell of his salvation from day to day.

Declare his glory among the nations,
his marvelous works among all the peoples.

—Psalm 96:1–3

Texts

1. Now Sings My Soul a New Song

1. My soul, O Lord, your wondrous work beholds
and sings unending psalms of praise.
The boundless universe and all it holds
reveal the beauty of your ways.
Now sings my soul a new song of adoration, with all Creation.
Now sings my soul a new song, yes, a new song for the Lord!

2. My soul, O Lord, is breathing free once more,
for you unburdened it of sin.
In song, my gratitude and love outpour,
as grace and mercy flooded in.
Now sings my soul a new song, a proclamation of my salvation.
Now sings my soul a new song, yes, a new song for the Lord!

3. My soul, O Lord, cries out in joy today.
It dances in the morning dew.
The darkness of the night has passed away.
Your light is making all things new.
Now sings my soul a new song, a celebration of transformation.
Now sings my soul a new song, yes, a new song for the Lord!

4. My soul, O Lord, is deeply moved to share
good news of all your grace has done,
to join my voice with people everywhere,
the many praising you as one.
Now sings my soul a new song, an invitation to congregation.
Now sings my soul a new song, yes, a new song for the Lord!

Themes/occasions: Praise. Creation. Redemption. Salvation. Unity. Music. Renewal. Invitation. Community of faith. Morning. Light. Grace. Christian witness. Freedom.

Scripture suggestions: 2 Corinthians 5:14–21. Psalm 33. Psalm 96. Psalm 98. Psalm 100. Psalm 149. Psalm 150. Ephesians 5:18–20. Matthew 11:28–30. Isaiah 42:9–12. Isaiah 43:18–19. Revelation 21:1–5. Romans 6:20–23. Romans 8:1–2. Romans 10:13–15.

Musical setting: EL NATHAN, alt.

2. Mary, You're the Chosen One

1. Mary, you're the chosen one
to give birth to God's own son—
you, a humble Jewish girl;
he, the savior of the world. *R.*

R. Oh, never fear, and never doubt!
Almighty God can bring about
the wondrous things he promised to you.
Some day they'll all come true.

2. Mary, you will be called blessed,
honored high above the rest.
Generations yet to come
will bow down before your son. *R.*

3. Mary, mothering this boy
will bring pain as well as joy.
Help prepare him to fulfill
God the Father's perfect will. *R.*

4. Mary, weeping at the cross
for the precious child you've lost,
be at peace and understand
that his death is in God's plan. *R.*

Themes/occasions: The Annunciation. Mary (mother of Jesus). Christmas. Advent. Holy Week. Mother's Day. Calvary. God's will. God's plan. God's promises. Father God.

Scripture suggestions: Luke 1:26–38. Luke 2:1–20. Luke 2:41–52. Matthew 1:18–25. John 19:25–27.

Musical setting: SOMEDAY, alt.

3.   The Son of God Is Coming

1. The Son of God is coming! He's going to be here soon,
just as the angel promised: born of a virgin's womb.
Clean house to show him honor. With water, soap, and broom,
scrub every nook and corner. Make ready every room.

2. The Son of God is coming, perhaps this very day!
Will our reception please him or turn him sad away?
With doors and hearts thrown open, let's greet our guest and say,
"Please make yourself at home here. We want you, Lord, to stay!"

3. The Son of God is coming! The kingdom's gracious heir
will dwell among his people in answer to their prayer.
Let those who have abundance be generous and share,
so each and every one may a joyful feast prepare.

4. The Son of God is coming! The skies reverberate
with angel choirs announcing the end of our long wait!
At last, he's on his way here. Come on! Don't hesitate!
Let's run and meet our Savior! It's time to celebrate!

Themes/occasions: Advent. Christmas. Preparation. Jesus Christ's return.
Waiting.
Scripture suggestions: Luke 1:26–35. Luke 12:35–40. Matthew 3.
Matthew 16:27. Matthew 24:30–31. Matthew 24:36–44. Matthew 25:1–13.
Matthew 25:31–40. John 1:1–18.
Musical setting: LANCASHIRE

4. How Long Is the Longest Night

1. How long is the longest night?
How distant is the dawn?
It seems that time has ceased its flight
and hope for change is gone.
But wait! My God's strong hand
rules over time and space!
At just the moment God has planned,
all things move into place!

2. How dark is the darkest day,
how black the shadow's gloom?
The richest colors fade to gray
when joy gives way to doom.
But wait! My God is light!
More vivid than the sun,
the face of Jesus Christ shines bright
with love for everyone!

3. How deep is the deepest fear?
How far can one soul fall?
The chasm's edge is oh, so near,
so close to claiming all!
But wait! My God has wings!
The Spirit lifts me high
above the pit of fearsome things
to soar beyond the sky!

Themes/occasions: Blue Christmas. Adversity. Hope. Trinity. God's plan.
God's presence. Light. The Transfiguration. Holy Spirit. Sovereign Lord.
Mental illness.

Scripture suggestions: Psalm 30:5. Psalm 89:5–14. Matthew 17:1–2.
John 8:12. Luke 1:78–79. Isaiah 40:28–31. Exodus 19:4. Romans 8:28.
Deuteronomy 32:8–13. Habakkuk 2:3. Habakkuk 3:17–19. Ephesians 1:9–11.
2 Corinthians 4:4–6. .

Musical setting: DIADEMATA, alt.

5. Roll Out the Red Carpet

1. Roll out the red carpet for this world premiere!
The star we've been longing for soon will appear.
The wise ones have followed his rising career.
Excitement is building, for curtain time's near!

2. His coming was promised, so all day and night
the faithful have waited to catch their first sight.
Now Jesus, whom heralds have called a Great Light,
approaches the stage, and the setting shines bright.

3. His entrance is humble, not pompous or proud.
The scene: a small stable with donkeys and cows.
No barriers hold back the worshipful crowd.
Poor shepherds and visiting kings are allowed.

4. This Jesus is destined for great leading roles
as teacher and healer who makes sinners whole,
forgiver of sins and dear friend who consoles.
He'll win crowning glory as savior of souls.

Themes/occasions: Christmas. Christmas Eve. Advent.
Scripture suggestions: Isaiah 9:2–7. Luke 2:1–20. Matthew 1:18–25.
Matthew 2:1–12.
Musical setting: MUELLER (AWAY IN A MANGER)

6. Mary's Lullaby

1. Welcome to the world, O heaven's promised heir!
You are the living proof of God's unfailing care,
a gracious gift in answer to his people's prayer,
the Savior who will free us from the sin we bear.

2. Welcome to my arms, O tiny child of grace,
enfolded in a warm and tender resting place.
Delight me with the look of love upon your face,
and satisfy your hunger here in my embrace.

3. Welcome to my heart, O precious little one!
I've waited, oh so eagerly, for you to come.
Tonight I look with joy at what the Lord has done
and ponder what tomorrow holds for you, my son.

4. (Coda) Now close your eyes, and have no fear.
The Lord and I are always near.
Welcome, Love. Welcome, Peace.
Welcome, Hope. Welcome, Jesus.

Themes/occasions: Christmas. Christmas Eve. Mary (mother of Jesus). God's promises.
Scripture suggestions: Luke 2:1–20. Matthew 1:18–25. Isaiah 9:2–7.
Musical setting: BONNEY

7. A Guardian's Prayer (Joseph's Song)

1. One Father in heaven, one father on earth
have waited with joy for our precious son's birth.
Not child of my body but child of my heart,
today our new life as a family will start.

2. My hands are so clumsy, all callused and rough;
to cuddle a baby, not gentle enough.
But I'll show him daily how deeply I care.
Whenever he needs me, he'll find me right there.

Gracious God, you've entrusted a treasure to me,
to protect, to provide, and to guide righteously.
I promise to cherish this child as my own
and to father him lovingly till he is grown.

3. Lord, you in your infinite mercy supplied
a woman to love and to work by my side.
Because she believed in your word, she was blessed
to give wondrous life to the babe at her breast.

4. The road to this place has been painful and long.
Now I must resolve to stay faithful and strong.
The journey from here full of hardship may be,
but you and my family are counting on me.

Gracious God, you've entrusted a treasure to me,
to protect, to provide, and to guide righteously.
A job too demanding for one simple man!
Father, help me to be the best father I can.

Themes/occasions: Christmas. Christmas Eve. Father's Day. Father God.
Family. God's promises. Adoption of a child. Joseph (father of Jesus). Trust.
Baptisms. Faith. Service. God's power and protection.
Scripture suggestions: Luke 2:1–20. Matthew 1:18–25. Isaiah 9:2–7.
Musical setting: TO GOD BE THE GLORY, alt.

8. A New Father's Prayer

1. One Father in heaven, one father on earth
have waited with joy for our precious child's birth.
Both child of my body and child of my heart,
today our new life as a family will start.

2. My hands are so clumsy, all callused and rough;
to cuddle a baby, not gentle enough.
But I'll show her/him daily how deeply I care.
Whenever she/he needs me, she'll/he'll find me right there.

Gracious God, you've entrusted a treasure to me,
to protect, to provide, and to guide righteously.
I promise to give her/him the same love you've shown
and to father her/him lovingly till she/he is grown.

3. Lord, you in your infinite mercy supplied
a woman to love and to work by my side.
Because she believed in your word, she was blessed
to give wondrous life to the babe at her breast.

4. The road to this place has been painful and long.
Now I must resolve to stay faithful and strong.
The journey from here full of hardship may be,
but you and my family are counting on me.

Gracious God, you've entrusted a treasure to me,
to protect, to provide, and to guide righteously.
A job too demanding for one simple man!
Father, help me to be the best father I can.

Themes/occasions: Christmas. Christmas Eve. Father's Day. Father God.
Family. Trust. God's provision. Baptisms. Faith. God's power and protection.
Scripture suggestions: Luke 2:1–20. Matthew 1:18–25. Isaiah 9:2–7.
Musical setting: TO GOD BE THE GLORY, alt.

9. Greet Your Savior

1. Set the candles aflame!
Lift your eyes and rejoice,
faces bright with good cheer Christmas morn!
Let the nations proclaim
in a jubilant voice
that the Light of the World has been born! *R.*

R. Hallelujah! Glad people, arise!
As the heavenly host fills the skies
with resounding good news of great joy,
greet your savior, God's own baby boy!

2. Ring the church bells and chimes
in the crisp morning air!
Read the stories we all love so well.
Sing the carols and rhymes.
Join in worship and prayer,
for the Lord came among us to dwell! *R.*

3. Wrap with ribbons and bows
gifts for people you love,
as the Christ child embraced humble birth
wrapped in swaddling clothes
as a gift from above,
beyond price, for all people on earth! *R.*

Themes/occasions: Christmas. Epiphany. Seeker. Praise. God's presence.
Father God. Light.
Scripture suggestions: Luke 1:78–79. Luke 2:1–20. Matthew 1:18–23.
John 8:12.
Musical setting: OLD RUGGED CROSS

10. Indigo Christmas

1. The indigo of twilight deepens fast
to darkness as I dwell upon the past.
The festive Christmas season is here,
but I feel only loneliness and fear.
O Lord, my Lord! Do you still hear my cries?
I long for you to come and dry my eyes.

2. Loud strains of Christmas music fill the air,
bright lights and cheerful colors everywhere,
gifts tied with ribbons red, gold, and green.
I'm bound with cords of blue that can't be seen.
O Lord, my Lord! If truly you love me,
come soon and set my grieving spirit free.

3. A silent swirl of snow falls in the night.
The landscape dons a cloak of sparkling white,
but my world wears a dull, dismal hue,
for sorrow dyes my days a dreary blue.
O Lord, my Lord! How long shall I be sad?
Bring back the hopeful heart that I once had.

4. I think about that night in Bethlehem.
No jolly songs, no Christmas lights for them!
Despair and darkness shrouded the earth.
Yet joy arrived, with baby Jesus' birth!
O Lord, my Lord! Come now, as you came then!
O Light of Life, be born in me again!

Themes/occasions: Christmas. Blue Christmas. Advent. Hope. Waiting. Loss.
Mourning. God's presence. Light.
Scripture suggestions: Luke 2:1–38. Matthew 1:18–2:23.
Musical setting: VENI EMMANUEL, alt.

11. Are You Seeking the Christ

1. Are you seeking the Christ? Will you leave all your sheep
and at once run to find him, while others still sleep?
Will you shout your good news to a world dark and cold
that a savior is born as the prophets foretold?

2. Are you seeking the Christ? Will you follow his star
to wherever it leads you, no matter how far?
Will you journey for years in your quest for the king?
Will you bow low before him? What gift will you bring?

3. Are you seeking the Christ? Do you ask for a sign?
Have you not seen the one who gives sight to the blind?
How he cures the afflicted and raises the dead?
How his gospel to both rich and poor ones is said?

4. Are you seeking the Christ? Dare you draw near the cross
on the Calvary hill, where his lifeblood was lost?
Will you go to the garden, examine his tomb,
and believe he appeared in the locked upper room?

5. Are you seeking the Christ? Why gaze up at the sky?
He's not there! He has gone to his kingdom on high!
Will you seek him in glory? Yes, there you shall meet!
Cease your searching, and lay all you have at his feet!

Themes/occasions: Christmas. Epiphany. The upper room. Ascension.
Seeker. Eternal life. Calvary. Easter. Jesus Christ's ministry and miracles.
Christ the King.
Scripture suggestions: Jeremiah 29:11–14. Luke 2:8–20. Luke 7:18–22.
Matthew 2:1–12. Matthew 11:2–5. John 20:1–18. Acts 1:9–11.
Musical setting: FOUNDATION

12. I Climbed the Mountain Heights to Pray

1. I climbed the mountain heights to pray
with Jesus Christ, one wondrous day.
His face like sun began to shine,
transfigured by a light divine.
Elijah joined him, Moses too.
They talked with him as old friends do.
They cheered him on to do God's will,
the Law and Prophets to fulfill.

2. Above, from in a shining cloud,
a voice declared, so clear and loud,
"This is my Son, whom I love well."
In awe, upon my face I fell.
How good it was to be there then!
But Jesus led me down again,
for in the valley must be done
the work God asks of everyone.

Themes/occasions: The Transfiguration. Light. Obedience. Jesus Christ's
ministry and miracles. Moses. Elijah.

Scripture suggestions: Matthew 5:17. Matthew 17:1–13. Mark 9:2–13.
2 Peter 1:16–18. 2 Corinthians 4:4–6.

Musical setting: SWEET HOUR

13. We Climbed the Heights with Christ to Pray

1. We climbed the heights with Christ to pray,
and on the mountaintop that day
we saw the face of Jesus shine,
transfigured by a light divine.

2. Moses appeared, Elijah too.
They talked with him as old friends do.
They cheered him on to do God's will,
the Law and Prophets to fulfill.

3. High, from inside a bright, dense cloud,
a voice declared, so clear and loud,
"This is my Son, whom I love well."
In awe, upon our knees we fell.

4. How good it was to be there then!
But Jesus led us down again,
for in the valley must be done
the work God asks of everyone.

Themes/occasions: The Transfiguration. Light. Obedience. Jesus Christ's ministry and miracles. Moses. Elijah.
Scripture suggestions: Matthew 5:17. Matthew 17:1–13. Mark 9:2–13. 2 Peter 1:16–18. 2 Corinthians 4:4–6.
Musical setting: TRURO

14. With Jesus on a Mountain

1. With Jesus on a mountain stood Peter, James, and John.
Strange light beamed from within him, while they, in awe, looked on.
As he prayed, the face of Jesus shone like sun, so pure and bright,
and the clothing he was wearing became a dazzling white.
Could his transfiguration be heaven's sacred sign
that Jesus, the Messiah, was given power divine?

2. Then Moses and Elijah the prophet stood there too.
They talked a while with Jesus, the way that old friends do.
Did the wondrous conversation that the three disciples saw
prove that Jesus satisfied both the Prophets and the Law?
"How good it is to be here!" the rest heard Peter say.
"Lord, let me build three shelters, where each of you can stay."

3. While Peter was still speaking, above them shone a cloud.
A voice from deep inside it spoke very clear and loud:
"This is my beloved Son, and what he says, be sure you hear."
At these words, the three disciples fell to the ground in fear.
Who made that declaration? they wondered, overawed.
Had Jesus just been claimed as the holy Son of God?

Themes/occasions: The Transfiguration. Light. Jesus Christ's ministry and
miracles. Moses. Elijah. The apostles.
Scripture suggestions: Matthew 5:17. Matthew 17:1–13. Mark 9:2–13.
2 Corinthians 4:4–6. 2 Peter 1:16–18.
Musical setting: THAXTED

15. Come, Gather at the Table

1. Come, gather at the table! The feast of love is spread.
Recall how Jesus gave thanks, blessed wine, and broke the bread
while knowing that tomorrow he'd hear the mob's cruel shout.
His body would be broken. His blood would be poured out. *R.*

R. Come, gather at the table as often as you're able.
Come, gather at the table for comfort, strength, and love.

2. Come, gather at the table to share the sacred meal,
for by his blood and body our souls are fed and healed.
In times of trial and trouble, hold one another close,
as Christ that night found solace with those he loved the most. *R.*

3. Come, gather at the table, no matter what your sin.
The host of this communion invites the sinner in.
Remember that he offered the loaf and cup of grace
to all who sat beside him. So come, and take your place! *R.*

Themes/occasions: Maundy Thursday. Holy Communion. Holy Week.
Redemption. Community of faith. Remembrance. Invitation. Comfort.
Scripture suggestions: Matthew 26:20–30. Mark 14:17–24. Luke 22:14–20.
Acts 2:42–47.
Musical setting: HANKEY

16. Break the Loaf

1. Break the loaf, as I bow my head
and echo the words of blessing you said.
O body that for love of me bled!
O Jesus Christ, the life-giving bread!

2. Lift the cup of lasting accord.
Thank God by whose grace our souls are restored.
O blood for our salvation outpoured!
O Jesus Christ, our savior and Lord!

3. Pass the gift from your hand to mine:
a morsel of bread, a sweet taste of wine.
O sacred blood! O body divine!
O Jesus Christ, love's tangible sign!

Themes/occasions: Maundy Thursday. Holy Communion. Holy Week. Lent.
Redemption. Renewal. Community of faith. God's presence. Jesus Christ's
ministry and miracles. Covenant renewal. Salvation.

Scripture suggestions: Matthew 26:20–30. Mark 14:17–24. Luke 22:14–20.
John 6:30–58. 1 Corinthians 10:16–17. 1 Corinthians 11:23–26.

Musical setting: BREAK THE LOAF

17.   Before Us, Alive

1. How we grieved when we heard that our Master had died,
how the nails tore his hands and the spear pierced his side!
Oh, the suff'ring he bore as he hung on the cross!
When his life ebbed away, our salvation seemed lost.
But our grief turned to joy, and our hope was revived,
when the One whom we mourned stood before us, alive.

2. In a locked upper room we sat huddled in fear.
All at once in our midst the Lord Jesus appeared!
Jesus raised from the dead? How could such a thing be?
Yet the marks of his wounds proved it really was he.
Then our grief turned to joy, and our hope was revived,
for the One whom we mourned stood before us, alive.

3. "Peace be with you," he said. "Blessed are all who believe,
for a life everlasting with me they'll receive.
Now, the marvels you've seen are a gift you must share.
Go, invite all the world to the home I'll prepare."
Yes, our grief turned to joy, and our hope was revived,
for the One whom we mourned stood before us, alive.

4. Look in God's Holy Word; see our witness to you.
By his spirit, believe what we know to be true:
With his anguish and death, Jesus paid for our sin.
Our redeemer lives now. Live forever with him.
Let your grief turn to joy and your hope be revived,
for the One who loves you stands before you, alive.

Themes/occasions: Sunday after Easter. The upper room. Resurrection.
Eternal life. The cross. Peace. The Great Commission. Faith. Holy Week.
Scripture suggestions: 1 John 2:1–2. John 20:19–29. John 14:1–3.
Musical setting: CHRISTMAS SONG, alt.

18, 19. If Jesus Christ Had Beckoned Me

1. If Jesus Christ had beckoned me to enter
the upper room the night he was betrayed
and said, "Come share my supper, dear repenter,"
I wonder now what choice I would have made.
Would I with joy his outstretched hand have taken,
the narrow steps at once begun to climb?
Or with a sigh, would I my head have shaken
and said, "I'm sorry, Lord. Perhaps some other time"?

2. If Jesus Christ had called me to the table
where his close friends already had reclined,
would I, a stranger there, have felt unable
to join the group that oft with Jesus dined?
Or, trusting him to smooth the way before me,
would I have boldly mingled with the rest
and found a place of welcome waiting for me
among the ones who knew and loved our host the best?

3. When Jesus Christ took bread, and blessed and broke it,
and said, "Behold my body! Take and eat,"
would I have claimed, the instant that he spoke it,
the offered loaf of sacramental wheat?
And when he raised the cup, gave thanks, and stated,
"This is my blood, the blood I shed for you,"
would I have eagerly my turn awaited
to drink the wine as he invited us to do?

4. The table's set. I hear his invitation:
"Come share the meal I suffered to prepare."
Now I will join, with great anticipation,
the fellowship of souls who gather there.
Lifelong disciples, yes, and new believers,
both young and old, all genders, every race,
both rich and poor, the dancers and the grievers
together eat the bread and drink the wine of grace.

4. *(Alternate)* The table's set. Do you hear Jesus call you
to share the meal he suffered to prepare?
Come now, and join this fellowship, for all who
accept his call find love and mercy there.
Lifelong disciples, yes, and new believers,
both young and old, all genders, every race,
both rich and poor, the dancers and the grievers:
Together, eat the bread and drink the wine of grace.

Themes/occasions: Holy Communion. Maundy Thursday. Invitation. Unity.
Community of faith. Jesus Christ's ministry and miracles. The upper room.
God's presence.

Scripture suggestions: Luke 22:7–19. Revelation 3:20. Revelation 19:9.
Mark 10:17–22. Mark 14:17–24. Matthew 22:1–14. Matthew 26:17–30.
Matthew 28:18–20. Acts 2:21.

Musical settings: LONDONDERRY AIR (#18); GLENDALE (#19)

20. O Redeemer, May Remembrance

1. O Redeemer, may remembrance of the covenant you seal
be renewed each time we join to celebrate your sacred meal.
We, the fellowship of faithful, come together in this place,
hungry for the gospel message, thirsty for your saving grace.

2. Son of God, you are the food that can sustain both flesh and soul.
When the loaf is blessed and broken, we who eat it are made whole.
With this bread of your pure body, given up to bear our shame,
fill us up with strength to live a life of service in your name.

3. Holy Savior, let the sweet communion wine we share today
linger long upon our lips to flavor every word we say.
From this chalice of your blood, poured out for pardon of our sin,
may forgiveness flow through us and hearts of mercy beat within.

4. Living Jesus, from your table send us forth refreshed and stirred
by the spirit to a deeper faith through sacrament and word.
May your presence in the precious bread and wine which we receive
be a taste of life eternal, for God's promise we believe!

Themes/occasions: Holy Communion. Maundy Thursday. Holy Week.
Remembrance. Eternal life. Forgiveness. Unity. Service. Redemption.
Renewal. Covenant renewal. Community of faith. God's promises.
Discipleship.

Scripture suggestions: Luke 22:7–19. Matthew 26:17–30. Mark 14:17–24.
John 6:30–58. Acts 2:42–47. Romans 5:8. Hebrews 10:23. 1 John 2:1–2.
1 Corinthians 10:16–17. 1 Corinthians 11:23–26.

Musical settings: MOUNT HOLYOKE; RUSTINGTON

21. Jesus Said Yes

1. "Son," said the Father God, "hear my request.
Will you be sacrificed and sinners be blessed:
Give up your honored place,
live with the human race?
Die, as my gift of grace?"
Jesus said yes.

2. Then came the evening of Jesus' arrest.
Knowing the trials to come and greatly distressed,
he prayed in agony
in dark Gethsemane.
He so loved you and me,
Jesus said yes.

3. "Father, please take away this fearsome test,
if that be possible. Yet, do what is best.
Your will, not mine, be done.
Finish what we've begun!"
cried the obedient one.
Jesus said yes.

Themes/occasions: Maundy Thursday. Holy Week. Good Friday. Lent.
God's commands.
Scripture suggestions: Philippians 2:5–8. Matthew 26:36–46. Mark 14:32–42.
Luke 22:40–46.
Musical setting: PROPIOR DEO, alt.

22, 23. The Uphill Road

1. Lord, you took upon your back the heavy cross of Calvary,
fully understanding where that rugged path was going to lead,
and in meek submission to your holy Father's sovereign will,
resolutely dragged your cross along the road that wound uphill.

2. Roughly jostled by a mob who pelted stones and loudly jeered,
stumbling over ruts and rocks it seemed at every turn appeared,
underneath the shifting weight of the unwieldy load you held,
Lord, you fixed your eyes upon the final goal that lay ahead.

3. Weakened by the brutal lash that many times your back had crossed,
you were worn out from the strain and fainting from the blood you'd lost.
In a fragile human body you had come to earth to dwell,
but that body's finite store of strength ran out, and down you fell.

4. Hands of pity touched your face to wipe the blood and sweat away.
Other hands reached out to haul you up and shove you on your way.
Minutes must have crawled like hours as you tried to keep the pace
to the spot they called Golgotha, to your execution place.

5. At the summit, you were nailed upon a cross of seeming shame,
but surrendering to death, you glorified your Father's name.
By your suffering and dying, scripture's promise was fulfilled.
Now you beckon me to walk that rugged road that winds uphill.

6. Lord, I took upon my back a heavy cross to follow you,
little understanding what that rugged path would lead me to.
In reluctant resignation to our holy Father's will,
now I slowly drag my cross along the road that winds uphill.

7. I'm discouraged by the jeers of those I thought to be my friends,
and I stumble on desire to follow selfish, worldly ends.
It's so hard to keep my balance underneath this weighty load!
I must fix my wand'ring eyes upon the One who chose this road.

8. Weakened by the painful trials that many times my path had crossed,
I am worn out from the strain and trying not to count the cost.
Lord, you know I'm only human, so it's no surprise at all
when my burden proves too much for my own strength, and down I fall.

9. Hands of pity touch my face to wipe my weary tears away.
Other hands reach out to lift me up and help me on my way.
Still, the minutes crawl like hours, but I can't speed up my pace,
just one foot before the other, toward some God-appointed place.

10. Lord, the road you've mapped for me may lead to loneliness and
    shame,
but if carrying this cross will serve to glorify your name,
I will bear it, in your footsteps, till your promise is fulfilled
of salvation at the summit of the road that winds uphill.

Themes/occasions: Calvary. Holy Week. Good Friday. The cross. Obedience.
God's commands. Lent. Salvation. God's promises.
Scripture suggestions: Luke 9:21–26. Luke 14:25–33. Luke 22:41–44.
John 19:1–30. Matthew 16:21–27. Philippians 2:5–11. Philippians 3:10–21.
1 John 2:1–6.
Musical settings: UPHILL ROAD (#22); NETTLETON, alt. (#23)

24. Where Were the Twelve When Jesus Died

1. Where were the twelve when Jesus died?
Did his disciples stand at Jesus' side
and linger near until the spear
had verified that Jesus died?

2. Yes, John was there when Jesus died.
John and the women saw him crucified.
They did not leave, though greatly grieved
and terrified, when Jesus died.

3. Was Peter there when Jesus died?
No, Simon Peter sat alone and cried.
He burned with shame, for Jesus' name
he'd thrice denied, when Jesus died.

4. Was Judas there when Jesus died?
No, the betrayer, torn by guilt inside
because his kiss had come to this,
a noose had tied when Jesus died.

5. Where were the rest when Jesus died?
All of them scattered, as he'd prophesied.
At his arrest, they thought it best
to run and hide when Jesus died.

Themes/occasions: Calvary. Holy Week. Good Friday. Lent. The cross.
The apostles.

Scripture suggestions: Matthew 26. Matthew 27:1–10. Mark 14. Luke 22.
John 18. John 19.

Musical setting: GERMANY

25. Where Were the Twelve When Jesus Died

1. Where were the twelve when Jesus died?
Did any see him crucified
and linger near until the spear
had verified that Jesus died?

2. Yes, John was there when Jesus died.
The women, too, stood by his side.
They did not leave, though greatly grieved
and terrified, when Jesus died.

3. Was Peter there when Jesus died?
No, Peter sat alone and cried.
He burned with shame, for Jesus' name
he'd thrice denied, when Jesus died.

4. Was Judas there when Jesus died?
No, he was torn by guilt inside
because his kiss had led to this.
A noose he tied when Jesus died.

5. Where were the rest when Jesus died?
All scattered, as he'd prophesied,
at his arrest. They thought it best
to run and hide when Jesus died.

Themes/occasions: Calvary. Holy Week. Good Friday. Lent. The cross.
The apostles.
Scripture suggestions: Matthew 26. Matthew 27:1–10. Mark 14. Luke 22.
John 18. John 19.
Musical setting: TALLIS' CANON (Round)

26.   Jesus, Please Remember Me

1. I do believe that you are he
whom prophets called the Promised One.
Though "King of Jews" the mockers see,
you're truly King of everyone.
And when your kingdom comes to be,
then, Jesus, please remember me.
O Jesus, please remember me!

2. For all my crimes, I know that I
deserve this cross of pain and shame.
But you were whipped and made to die,
though innocent of any blame.
Your name will soon be praised on high.
Then, Jesus, don't forget my cry.
O Jesus, don't forget my cry!

3. What strange compassion you have shown,
to say we'll meet in paradise!
I hear a cry ... a dying groan ...
So, finished is your sacrifice.
Now, Jesus, are you on your throne?
Then number me among your own.
Oh, number me among your own!

I trust in you to set me free.
Have mercy, and remember me.
O Jesus, please remember me!

Themes/occasions: Good Friday. Lent. Holy Week. The cross. Remembrance. Christ the King. Redemption. Death and dying.
Scripture suggestions: Luke 23:40–43. Isaiah 49:15.
Musical setting: SOLID ROCK

27. Cross of Calvary

1. Cross of sin and cross of restoration!
Christ—himself forsaken—brought
sinners into reconciliation
with the just and holy God. *R.*

R. Sacrificed for our salvation, Jesus won the victory,
dying on the cross of Calvary.

2. Cross of death and cross of life unending!
"It is finished!" Jesus cried.
Thus he paid the price for our offending.
We shall live because he died. *R.*

3. Cross of shame and cross of kingdom glory!
Multitudes of souls to save,
Jesus suffered agony before he
rose in triumph from the grave. *R.*

Themes/occasions: Holy Week. Redemption. The cross. Good Friday. Easter.
Christ the King. Eternal life.

Scripture suggestions: 1 John 2:1–2. 1 Corinthians 1:17–31. Romans 5:10.
Hebrews 12:1–2. Isaiah 53.

Musical setting: CWM RHONDDA

28. God Loved the World

1. God loved the world so much his son he gave,
not to condemn but graciously to save.
What clear proof of
his all-forgiving love!
Alleluia! Alleluia!

2. God loved the world, not some but every one.
For all, he sent to death his only son.
With arms spread wide
was Jesus crucified.
Alleluia! Alleluia!

3. God loves the world! Shall we not do the same:
(SN) forgive and love all people in his name?
(S) love and forgive all people in his name?
Each one we meet,
with open arms let's greet!
Alleluia! Alleluia!

Themes/occasions: God's love. Love for neighbor. The cross. Forgiveness.
Acceptance of others. Calvary. Salvation.

Scripture suggestions: John 3:16–18. John 4:5–14. John 13:34–35.
Ephesians 3:14–21. Ephesians 4:31–32. Mark 12:30. Jeremiah 31:3.
Luke 10:27. 1 John 2:1–2.

Musical settings: SINE NOMINE; SARUM

29. As Droughty Clouds

1. As droughty clouds clutch to their bosoms
    precious drops of prayed-for rain
and offer only empty shadows
    to the dry and dusty plain,
would you, O God, hear fervent prayers,
    yet your precious grace withhold?
No, you rain blessings down in showers
    on my dry and dusty soul.

2. As thrifty farmers seek the richest
    soil to till and sow their seeds,
expecting there a greater harvest
    than among the rocks and weeds,
would you, O God, see all my sins and
    choose instead more fertile fields?
No! Harrow out my weeds and stones, then
    sow your love and reap your yields.

3. As bolted doors allow to enter
    only those who hold the keys,
and gates are locked against the ones who
    can't afford admission fees,
would you, O God, bar me from glory
    when the price I cannot pay?
No, Christ already paid it for me.
    I shall not be turned away.

Themes/occasions: Grace. God's provision. Discipleship. Salvation. Heaven. Redemption. Hope.Covenant renewal. God's faithfulness. Judgment. Good Friday. Nature. Ordinations. Praise.

Scripture suggestions: 1 Timothy 1:12–16. 1 Peter 3:18–22. 2 Samuel 23:1–4. Psalm 63:1–5. Jeremiah 17:5–8. Hebrews 10:10–17. 2 Corinthians 9:7–15. Proverbs 25:14. Mark 2:13–17. Luke 5:27–32. Matthew 9:9–13. John 3:16–18. Jude 1:24–25.

Musical setting: CONVERSE, alt.

30. Roll the Stone Away

1. Jesus, with the dawning, roll away our gloom,
1.* *Lord, this Easter morning, roll away our gloom,*
for your dying ends in triumph, not in doom.
There's no need for tears or burial perfume.
When the stone is rolled away, there stands an empty tomb! *R.*

R. Show the world today, O Lord! Show the world today!
Show your risen glory! Roll the stone away!

2. Roll away the curtain from our point of view.
Open up our eyes to what God's pow'r can do.
With the rising sun, we see you risen too.
When the stone is rolled away, we find the living you! *R.*

3. Roll away the traces of our pardoned sin.
Clear the way for grace and love to grow within.
Seeking to be holy, claiming Christ as kin,
when the stone is rolled away, new life we shall begin. *R.*

4. Roll away our questions, every ling'ring doubt.
Let the light of truth in. Chase the darkness out.
Hear more voices joining, eager and devout.
When the stone is rolled away, we'll raise a joyful shout! *R.*

*Easter Sunday

Themes/occasions: Easter. Resurrection. Renewal. Grace. Light. Truth. Holiness.
Scripture suggestions: Luke 24:1–12. Matthew 28:1–8. John 20:1–10. 2 Corinthians 4:4–6. Mark 16:1–8. 1 John 5:1–5. Revelation 12:10.
Musical setting: ST. GERTRUDE

31.   Lean on God

1. Lean on God in times of sorrow.
All his strength is yours to borrow.
He will hold you, till tomorrow
brings a clearer, brighter, gladder day.

2. Give your heart and soul to Jesus
when they lie in painful pieces.
When at last your weeping ceases,
he'll wipe every bitter tear away.

3. Seek the guidance of the Spirit.
You will know it when you hear it.
Greet the future; never fear it,
for the Spirit knows the better way.

4. Share your burdens with the faithful.
Lighten theirs, if you are able.
Then join hands around the table
and together bow your heads and pray.

Themes/occasions: Adversity. Trinity. Holy Spirit. Comfort. Unity.
Community of faith. Prayer. God's presence.
Scripture suggestions: Revelation 21:1–4. Daniel 10:19. 1 Corinthians 12:31.
2 Corinthians 7:10. 2 Corinthians 12:9. Exodus 4:31. Habakkuk 3:17–19.
1 Chronicles 16:11. Philippians 4:4–9. Philippians 4:13.
Musical setting: NORRIS, alt.

32. May My Footprints on Your Heart

1. May my footprints on your heart be deep but gently laid,
and remembrance of my presence never fully fade.
May your heart be ever warmed
by the bond of love we formed
and be comforted each day by memories we made.

2. May my footprints on your mind inspire and challenge you
to stand up for what is just and cling to what is true.
When the truth seems lost or blurred,
let the echo of my word
help you find the way that's good and guide you safely through.

3. May my footprints on your soul shine bright, an inward sign
that indeed the things of earth and heaven intertwine,
giving hope one day you'll be
with our Father God and me,
all together for all time, to live in realms divine.

Themes/occasions: Ascension. Funerals and memorials. Departures. Love.
Death and dying. God's presence. Eternal life. Heaven. Remembrance.
Discipleship. Guidance. Justice. Father God.

Scripture suggestions: Philippians 4:9. Matthew 5:15–16. Matthew 28:18–20.
John 14:18–19. Luke 22:19. 2 Timothy 1:3–5. Hebrews 11:1–12:1.
1 Thessalonians 4:13–18. Acts 1:6–11.

Musical setting: DIVINE MYSTERIES, alt.

33.   My Footprints on Your Life

1. May my footprints on your heart be deep but gently laid,
and remembrance of my presence never fully fade.
May your heart be ever warmed
by the bond of love we formed
and be comforted each day by memories we made.

2. May my footprints on your mind inspire and challenge you
to stand up for what is just and cling to what is true.
When the truth seems lost or blurred,
let the echo of my word
help you find the way that's good and guide you safely through.

3. May my footprints on your soul shine bright, an inward sign
that indeed the things of earth and heaven intertwine,
giving hope one day you'll be
with our Father God and me,
all together for all time, to live in realms divine.

Look inside yourself and see
marks that bind, yet set you free,
after I have said goodbye: my footprints on your life.

Themes/occasions: Ascension. Funerals and memorials. Departures. Love.
Death and dying. God's presence. Eternal life. Heaven. Remembrance.
Discipleship. Guidance. Justice. Father God.

Scripture suggestions: Philippians 4:9. Matthew 5:15–16. Matthew 28:18–20.
John 14:18–19. Luke 22:19. 2 Timothy 1:3–5. Hebrews 11:1–12:1.
1 Thessalonians 4:13–18. Acts 1:6–11.

Musical setting: KELVINGROVE, alt.

34. Jesus, in a Long-Ago Time

1. Jesus, in a long-ago time,
turned water into finest wine.
With just a touch and a few words said,
he waked a young girl from the dead.

2. Jesus healed the sick and the blind
and with the outcasts gladly dined.
Five thousand people one day he fed
with two small fishes and some bread.

3. Poor folk found that Jesus was kind.
To hypocrites he spoke his mind.
Across the land Jesus' teaching spread:
Give up your sins; love God instead.

4. Jewish leaders asked for a sign
to prove his mission was divine.
His frightened followers quickly fled
when to Golgotha he was led.

5. Though he had committed no crime,
he paid the price for yours and mine.
Upon a cross Jesus hung and bled
until his last drop had been shed.

6. Three days later, no one could find
his body where it had reclined.
Inside the tomb, where they'd laid his head,
his burial linens lay instead.

7. Jesus rules a kingdom sublime
today and till the end of time.
Eternal life we've inherited,
for he is risen from the dead.

Optional Refrain: Yes, so the Bible said.

Themes/occasions: Jesus Christ's ministry and miracles. Christ the King.
Resurrection. The Bible.

Scripture suggestions : John 2:1–11. John 2:13–25. John 6:1–14. John 9:1–41.
John 19:16–37. John 19:38–20:10. Mark 2:1–12. Mark 2:13–17. Mark 5:22–43.
Mark 6:35–44. Mark 8:1–9. Mark 8:22–25. Mark 10:46–52. Mark 14:50.
Mark 15:24–38. Mark 15:42–16:8. Matthew 8:1–16. Matthew 9:1–13.
Matthew 9:18–26. Matthew 12:38–45. Matthew 14:13–21. Matthew 15:32–39.
Matthew 16:1–4. Matthew 23:1–33. Matthew 26:46–56. Matthew 27:26–50.
Matthew 27:57–28:15. Galatians 3:13–14. Luke 5:27–32. Luke 8:41–56.
Luke 9:10–17. Luke 17:11–19. Luke 18:35–43. Ephesians 1:7. 1 John 2:1–2.
Revelation 12:10.

Musical setting: ORIENTIS PARTIBUS, alt.

35. What Are You Fishing For

1. What are you fishing for?
What do you hope to catch?
Lay down your nets
with no regrets,
and souls you'll fetch. *R.*

R. Leave all behind!
Leave work and war and worried mind,
and follow Christ!

2. What are you fighting for?
Who are your enemies?
Lay down your sword,
and serve the Lord
in grace and peace. *R.*

3. What are you fretting for?
What task? What pressing need?
Lay down your care
at once and dare
to let Christ lead. *R.*

4. What are you falt'ring for?
When he calls "Come with me,"
be on your way
without delay
to ministry. *R.*

Themes/occasions: Invitation. Ministry and outreach. Service. Discipleship.
Scripture suggestions: Matthew 4:18–22. Matthew 16:23–25. Matthew 19:16–22. Mark 1:16–18. Mark 10:17–27. Luke 5:27–28. Luke 10:38–42. Luke 18:18–23. John 1:35–44. John 18:1–16.
Musical setting: DARWALL'S 148th

36. O Lord, We Are Grateful

1. O Lord, we are grateful for all that you give:
a bounty of blessings each day that we live.
No one can outgive you. Your grace knows no bounds.
Heaped up, overflowing, your measure astounds.

2. How fitting and joyful on this day of days
to pause and reflect on your generous ways!
Help us be as gracious in thought, word, and deed
and open our hands to all neighbors in need.

3. Remind us to never consider our due
the talents and treasure that flow, Lord, from you.
Good stewards of riches on earth we will be
and sing thankful praises for eternity.

Themes/occasions: Thanksgiving. Church milestones. Dedications.
Stewardship. Love for neighbor. God's provision. Ministry and outreach.
Grace. Hospitality.
Scripture suggestions: Ephesians 3:14–21. Matthew 25:40. 1 Peter 4:10.
Luke 6:34–38. Psalm 100. Esther 4:6–17.
Musical setting: ST. DENIO

37. Seasons

1. In the season of spring,
nature rises anew.
From the treetops birds sing,
giving glory to you.
Every part of creation
on heaven and earth
joins a glad celebration—
your gift of new birth!

2. Through the summer's long days,
we say thanks as we toil
for your sun's cheerful rays
and your rain on the soil.
It's the season of growing
and seeking your will,
for in finding and knowing
you we are fulfilled.

3. When the autumn leaves fall,
then we reap what was sown,
praising you for it all,
for the bounty you've shown.
On the threshing room floor,
chaff will be blown away;
weeds will flourish no more,
after your harvest day.

4. As the weather turns cold
and the winter sets in,
though we're weary and old,
we can't wait to begin
the next season of life,
in this world or beyond,
for your gift of new life,
Lord, forever goes on.

Themes/occasions: Nature. Creation. God's will. Renewal. Eternal life. Faith.
Thanksgiving. Judgment.
Scripture suggestions: 2 Corinthians 5:14–21. Genesis 1:14–15. Ecclesiastes
3:1–13. Matthew 3:11–12. Matthew 13:24–30. Matthew 13:36–43.
Galatians 6:7–10. Luke 3:16–17.
Musical setting: CHRISTMAS SONG

38. People of God Keep Grumbling

R. Why do people of God keep grumbling, grumbling,
moaning and groaning, mumbling, mumbling?
God's great pow'r should be humbling, humbling,
but people of God keep grumbling, grumbling.

1. Oh, the Hebrew slaves were grumbling.
Their Egyptian bondage was cruel.
When the Lord called Moses to rescue them,
Moses started grumbling too.
"Lord, you know my speech is fumbling.
Why should Pharaoh listen to me?"
But the Lord helped Moses, and finally
Pharaoh let the Hebrews go free.

2. But the Hebrews did more grumbling
when the pharaoh's army gave chase.
'Tween Egyptian chariots and the sea,
they were in a desperate place.
The Egyptians all went tumbling.
In the sea their army was drowned.
Moses split the waters by God's command,
and the Hebrews crossed on dry ground.

3. Soon the Hebrews started grumbling,
"There's no drinking water out here!"
Then the Lord said, "Moses, go strike that rock,"
and a stream of water flowed clear.
But they heard their bellies rumbling.
"Take us back to Egypt," they cried.
So the Lord, in answer to their demands,
quail and manna kindly supplied.

4. Yet the Hebrews went on grumbling.
Moses left, and rebels grew bold.
While the Lord wrote laws on a block of stone,
they adored a calf made of gold.
Moses saw their faith was crumbling,
and he begged the Lord to forgive.
Though he burned with anger, the Lord decreed
that his chosen people should live.

5. Still, the Hebrews kept on grumbling.
Spies came back from Canaan, afraid.
They did not believe they could conquer it,
so the Promised Land was delayed.
After forty years of stumbling
'round the desert, seemingly lost,
at the Jordan River they stood at last,
and the Lord God brought them across. *R.*

Themes/occasions: God's power and protection. God's provision. God's
faithfulness. Faith. Obedience. The Exodus.

Scripture suggestions: Exodus 1:6–22. Exodus 2:23–25. Exodus 3:7–12.
Exodus 4:10–17. Exodus 12:31–32. Exodus 14:1–31. Exodus 16:1–35.
Exodus 17:1–7. Exodus 32. Exodus 33:1–3. Numbers 13, 14. Joshua 3.
Deuteronomy 9:7–21.

Musical setting: GRUMBLING, alt.

39. You Didn't Just Give Us Light

1. You didn't just give us light,
you gave us colors,
a landscape drenched in every rainbow hue:
bright fireworks displays
and pastel mountain haze,
a daffodil, a blush, the heavens blue.

2. You didn't just give us sound,
you gave us music
to please the ear and stir our very soul:
a lilting lullaby,
a whistle or a sigh,
a symphony, a bell, a thunder roll.

3. You didn't just give us smell,
you gave us fragrance.
Aromas fill the air and pique the nose:
familiar smells of home,
a meadow freshly mown,
the piney woods, the perfume of a rose.

4. You didn't just give us food,
you gave us flavors
to tantalize our taste buds when we eat:
the creamy milk and cheese,
the savory fish and meats,
fresh bread, and juicy berries, tart or sweet.

5. You didn't just give us touch,
you gave us texture,
a world of objects interesting to feel:
small pebbles sharp and rough,
soft dandelion fluff,
warm kittens, flowing water, polished steel.

6. Not only are you our God,
you are our Father, *(you're our provider,)*
who showers us with blessings day by day.
Not only do you meet
our every daily need,
you do it in the most delightful way!

Themes/occasions: Creation. God's provision. Father God. Praise. Music. Thanksgiving. Nature. God's love. Father's Day.

Scripture suggestions: Psalm 104:24–28, 31. Psalm 100. 1 Timothy 6:17. Zephaniah 3:17. James 1:17. Ephesians 1:4–8. Matthew 7:9–11. Luke 11:11–13.

Musical setting: YOU DIDN'T JUST GIVE, alt.

40. Our Lives Are a Gift

1. Our lives are a gift bestowed by God,
a gift so sweet and good!
So let us raise
a song of praise
to show him our gratitude.

2. This life is a gift of joy from God
to use for his good will.
Then let us start,
with happy heart,
his purposes to fulfill.

3. All life is a gift conceived by God.
Each one whom he designed
let us protect;
for each, respect
the life span that he assigned.

4. Yes, life is a gift on earth from God,
who, in his wondrous love,
his promise kept.
Let us accept
his gift of new life above.

Themes/occasions: Thanksgiving. Sanctity of life. Eternal life. God's plan. God's provision. Praise. God's will. Service. God's love. Mother's Day.

Scripture suggestions: Psalm 139:13–16. Romans 6. Acts 17:24–28. Deuteronomy 12:28–31. Genesis 1:26–27. Isaiah 43:6b–7. Ecclesiastes 12. Jeremiah 1:4–5. Ephesians 2:10. Esther 4:6–17.

Musical setting: CRIMOND

41. You Will Live

1. Bones lay upon the ground,
dried out and scattered. No sign of life was found,
only the dead. Almighty God promised then,
"I will turn you back to living men,
give you flesh and muscle, cover them with skin."
When he breathed upon them, thousands lived again! *R.*

R. You will live! You will live!
Yes, the Lord says you will live!

2. "My little girl is ill,"
Jairus told Jesus. "Lord, if you only will,
come, make her well." Messengers said, "It's too late.
She is dead." But Jesus told him, "Wait!
Do not be afraid. Believe, and she'll be healed."
At his touch, the child got up and ate a meal! *R.*

3. Lazarus in the grave
four days lay buried. "Why didn't Jesus save
him?" people said. Finally, Jesus arrived.
He commanded, "Roll the stone aside!"
With a prayer, he called for Lazarus to rise,
and his friend walked out, to everyone's surprise! *R.*

Themes/occasions: Death and dying. Healing. Renewal. Lazarus. Jairus.
God's power and protection. Jesus Christ's ministry and miracles.
Scripture suggestions: Ezekiel 37:1–14. Matthew 9:18–19, 23–25.
Mark 5:22–24, 35–43. Luke 8:41–42, 49–56. John 11:1–44.
Musical setting: CHRIST AROSE

42.   A Lamb in the Wilderness

1. A lamb in the wilderness, lost and afraid,
too far from the Good Shepherd's flock I have strayed.
I long for his care, but I'm held back by shame.
Oh, listen! The shepherd is calling my name!
Here I am! Here I am! How I yearn to come home!
Here I am! Here I am! Nevermore will I roam.
He calls, and my spirit revives at the sound.
My shepherd kept searching until I was found.

2. Lord Jesus, you gave us your rod and your staff
to lead your flocks heavenward on your behalf.
But we have allowed them to wander in sin.
Forgive us, and help us to gather them in.
Here we stand! Here we stand, for your call we have heard.
Here we stand! Here we stand, to proclaim your true Word.
To feed and protect them we promise anew,
that every lamb someday may love and serve you.

3. As sheep know the sound of their own shepherd's voice,
your church hears you calling. We must make a choice:
run free, seeking grass that is greener we're told,
or humble ourselves and stay close to your fold.
Here we come! Here we come, back to where we belong.
Here we come! Here we come! In your will we are strong.
The sheep of your pasture, Lord, we choose to be.
Belonging to you we can be truly free.

4. Good Shepherd, we eagerly go where you lead
and trust you to give every good thing we need.
No lamb the wrong color, too big or too small—
your faithful provision encompasses all.
Here we sing! Here we sing, to our shepherd, the Lord.
Here we sing! Here we sing, now in joyful accord.
Renewed by the spirit, united in love,
we'll follow our shepherd to pastures above.

Themes/occasions: Good Shepherd. Ordinations. Covenant renewal. Holy
Spirit. Leadership. Redemption. Unity. Community of faith. Obedience.
God's provision. Invitation. Renewal. God's faithfulness. Freedom.
Scripture suggestions: Ezekiel 34. Jeremiah 23:1–6. Matthew 9:35–38.
Matthew 18:11–13. John 10:1–16. Psalm 23. 1 Timothy 1:12–16.
Musical setting: TO GOD BE THE GLORY

43. Are You Weary

1. Are you weary? Are you weak?
Cannot find the strength you seek?
Do you hunger? Do you thirst?
Search in vain your empty purse?
Turn to Jesus, by your side.
All you need he will provide.

2. Do you worry? Do you weep?
Does your pain cut sharp and deep?
Are you angry? Are you wronged?
Fought for justice far too long?
Jesus knows and understands.
Place your struggles in his hands.

3. Are you lonely? Are you lost?
Swept away and tempest-tossed?
Have you fallen? Have you failed?
Have your plans all been derailed?
Follow Jesus, now, today.
He's the life, the truth, the way.

Themes/occasions: Adversity. Justice. God's provision. Guidance. Invitation.
Comfort. Social conflict.
Scripture suggestions: Matthew 11:28–30. John 14:1–7. Psalm 94:15–23.
Psalm 120. 1 Peter 4. Habakkuk 1:2–4, 13. Habakkuk 3:17–19. 1 John 4:4–6.
1 John 5:1–5.
Musical setting: TOPLADY

44. God's People Share

1. God's people share what we possess
to meet the needs of those with less.
Come, you who leave your native land
to plant a future good and grand.
Here in our soil put down your roots
to bloom again on brave new shoots;
then share in turn your harvest fruits.

2. Where love begins, suspicion ends.
God's people smile and greet as friends
the ones who've moved from place to place
and seen distrust on every face.
Though we may dress or eat or pray
or speak a very different way,
let's find our common ground today.

3. To those who flee from want or strife
to seek a safe and peaceful life,
let's offer sanctuary here,
removed from danger, far from fear.
No cry for help can we ignore.
God's people stand on freedom's shore
with open heart and open door.

Themes/occasions: Acceptance of others. Love for neighbor. Hospitality.
Social conflict. Peace.Freedom. Invitation. Justice. Pentecost. Service.
Stewardship. Unity. Ministry and outreach.

Scripture suggestions: 2 Corinthians 9:7–15. Acts 2:44–47. Hebrews 13:1–3.
Matthew 25:31–46. 1 Peter 4:8–9. Leviticus 19:33–34. Deuteronomy 10:18–19.
Zechariah 7:9. Ephesians 4:1–6. Isaiah 56:6–8. Esther 4:6–17.

Musical setting: SOLID ROCK

45. Arise, and Serve the Holy One

1. As I awake, I seem to hear
the Spirit whisper in my ear
an invitation, oh, so grand
to do the work that God has planned.
"Awake, and greet the morning sun!
Rejoice! A new day has begun.
Arise, and serve the Holy One!"

2. With silent words at break of dawn,
the Spirit calls to spur me on
to make this day a song of praise
to God, the maker of all days.
"Awake, and greet the morning sun!
Rejoice! A new day has begun.
Arise, and serve the Holy One!"

3. No longer must I be downcast
by sins and failures of the past.
Each day I'm free to start anew
the life the Spirit calls me to.
"Awake, and greet the morning sun!
Rejoice! A new day has begun.
Arise, and serve the Holy One!"

Themes/occasions: Morning. Invitation. Renewal. Holy Spirit. Praise. Service. Redemption. God's plan. Freedom.

Scripture suggestions: Isaiah 50:4. Romans 13:11–14. Psalm 118:24. Ephesians 3:14–21. Lamentations 3:21–23.

Musical setting: SOLID ROCK

46, 47. The Dawn Breaks on a Cloudless Morn

1. The dawn breaks on a cloudless morn,
revealing earth afresh reborn.
Night folds away her somber veil,
and day sweeps mist from wood and dale.
High o'er creation, God's great hand
flings light across the waking land.
Grace shines in every drop of dew.
Lord, you are making all things new.

2. When day has gray with storms begun,
through parting clouds reach rays of sun.
Sprouts rise where seeds have dormant lain,
aroused by brightness after rain.
So does God's radiant touch invite
each soul to grow into the Light.
A rainbow writes on clearing skies:
Lord, you are just, but kind and wise.

3. With each new morning, year by year,
old blossoms fade, new buds appear.
The streams and fields are rearranged.
The highest hills, in time, are changed.
But one thing in this world is sure:
God's word forever will endure.
All praise the faithful One above!
Lord, you are pure, unfailing love.

4. So black and long the nighttime seems.
Yet, in the east a soft light gleams.
"The morn is coming," trills the lark,
in faith that light shall conquer dark.
Yes, hope on the horizon glows,
for Jesus from the grave arose!
The night shall flee when Christ descends.
Lord, you are day that never ends.

Themes/occasions: Morning. Praise. Creation. Renewal. God's faithfulness. Invitation. Light. Easter. Resurrection. Jesus Christ's return. Nature. Grace. God's love.
Scripture suggestions: 2 Samuel 23:1–4 New International Version (NIV). Lamentations 3:19–26. Jeremiah 31:3. Isaiah 40:6–8. Psalm 36:5–9. Psalm 40:9–11. Psalm 46:1–7. Psalm 59:16–17. Psalm 119:89–91. 1 Thessalonians 4:16. 2 Corinthians 4:4–6. 2 Corinthians 5:16–18. Deuteronomy 7:9. Genesis 9:8–16. Ephesians 5:8–14. Habakkuk 3:3–4. Revelation 12:10.
Musical settings: SWEET HOUR (#46); CANDLER/YE BANKS AND BRAES (#47)

48. Because You Loved Me First

1. You are Alpha and Omega, the future and the past.
You created earth and heaven, magnificent and vast!
You're the Kingdom and the Glory, mighty Lord of all you see.
Yet you care for lowly creatures. The lowliest is me.
Your love found my soul and claimed it, my downward path reversed.
Now I cry, "My God, I love you!" because you loved me first.

2. You so loved the world that Jesus, your only son, you sent,
through his suffering and dying to save the penitent.
Thus in love was sinners' ransom paid in full to set them free.
Even then, you knew that one of those sinners would be me.
Your love drew me up and cleansed me. In grace I was immersed.
Now I cry, "My God, I love you!" because you loved me first.

3. As in spring refreshing showers rouse dormant seeds to sprout
and bright beams of summer sunshine coax buds to blossom out,
you revived my withered spirit with a love I'll never earn.
From a brimming heart, I offer all my love in return.
Your love fed my soul's deep hunger and quenched my spirit's thirst.
Now I cry, "My God, I love you!" because you loved me first.

4. You who planned my days and hours, who formed me in the womb,
have prepared a home eternal for me beyond the tomb.
Being loved and blessed so richly, how can I do any less
than to share with other people your love and graciousness?
Your love showed me how to love both the worthy and the worst.
Now I cry, "My God, I love you!" because you loved me first.

Themes/occasions: Grace. God's love. Love for God. Love for neighbor.
Praise. Redemption. Creation. Sovereign Lord. Renewal. Eternal life.
Acceptance of others. God's presence.
Scripture suggestions: 1 John 2:1–2. 1 John 4:7–21. John 3:16. Hosea 6:3.
Colossians 1:16–17. Psalm 8. Psalm 138. Psalm 139:13–16. Romans 5:6–11.
Revelation 21:6. Ephesians 1:4–10. Ephesians 3:14–21. Deuteronomy 7:9.
Jeremiah 31:3.
Musical setting: THAXTED, alt.

49. Deep Is the Love of God for Me

1. Deep is the love of God for me,
proven on Calvary:
merciful love that set me free.
Daily, new grace I see.

2. Easy is Jesus' name to say,
so hard to walk his way!
Help me to live his love each day,
Spirit of Truth, I pray.

Themes/occasions: God's love. Discipleship. Love for neighbor. Calvary. Salvation.

Scripture suggestions: John 3:16–18. John 4:5–14. John 13:34–35. John 14. Mark 12:30. Luke 10:27. Acts 2:21. 1 John 2:1–2. Ephesians 3:14–21. Ephesians 4:31–32. Jeremiah 31:3. Romans 6.

Musical setting: WINDSOR

50. Without Love

1. If I speak in tongues of angels,
without love, oh, without love,
if my prayer, sweet and strange, is
without love, oh, without love,
though I sing a spirit song,
I am just a sounding gong.
Into noise my message changes,
without love, oh, without love.

2. If I have prophetic power,
without love, oh, without love,
if I know the day and hour,
without love, oh, without love,
though deep myst'ries I explain
and my wisdom falls like rain,
I am but a passing shower,
without love, oh, without love.

3. If I give away my treasure,
without love, oh, without love,
if my bounty knows no measure,
without love, oh, without love,
though I offer to the poor
everything I own and more,
to the Lord I give no pleasure,
without love, oh, without love.

4. If to suff'ring I surrender,
without love, oh, without love,
if a martyr's death I render,
without love, oh, without love,
though for Jesus' sake I'm slain,
by my sacrifice I gain
no more share in heaven's splendor,
without love, oh, without love.

5. If my faith can move a mountain,
without love, oh, without love,
if my hope flows like a fountain,
without love, oh, without love,
though I fervently believe
life eternal I'll receive,
yet as nothing am I counted,
without love, oh, without love.

6. Faith and hope will ever be, as
always love, oh, always love.
But the greatest of these three is
always love, oh, always love.
So, let love surround and lift
use of every spirit gift
in the better way of Jesus:
always love. Oh, always love!

Themes/occasions: Love for neighbor. Spirit gifts. Love. Ministry and outreach.
Scripture suggestions: 1 Corinthians 12:31–13:3,13. 1 Peter 4:10–11.
Matthew 25:1–13.
Musical settings: HYMN TO JOY; IRBY, alt.; STAND BY ME

51. Growing Together

1. If your path leads to God *(Christ)*
and mine leads to him too,
then nearer you shall draw to me,
then nearer you shall draw to me,
and nearer I to you,
and nearer I to you. *R.*

R. We're growing together,
closer and closer together.
We'll grow much closer together
by both growing closer to God *(Christ).*

2. Put God *(Christ)* first in your life,
and I will do the same.
Then we shall share a bond of love,
then we shall share a bond of love,
united in his name,
united in his name. *R.*

3. If we should drift apart,
each going our own way,
reset your compass to the Lord,
reset your compass to the Lord.
We'll meet again one day.
We'll meet again one day. *R.*

Themes/occasions: Love for God. Sovereign Lord. Unity. Community of faith.
Scripture suggestions: Ephesians 4:1–7. John 17:21. Mark 12:30. Luke 10:27.
Matthew 6:33. 1 John 4:7. 1 Thessalonians 4:13–18.
Musical setting: MARCHING TO ZION

52.   Family Circle of God   (B/CF)

1. Look around your family circle. Are there breaks you ought to mend?
Have old quarrels made you enemies, instead of dearest friends?
Now's the time for you to find an olive branch you can extend.
Try! And let your family circle be unbroken once again.

2. Look around your inner circle. Do the people you hold dear
know how much you really love them? Have you made that message
    clear?
Share their sorrows and their joys. Confess your burdens and your fears.
Ties like these will bind your circle ever closer through the years.

3. Look around your widest circle. Does a biased pattern show?
Are the "different" folks not good enough for you to want to know?
Open up your heart and love them. Let your preconceptions go.
How much bigger can your circle then begin to stretch and grow!

4. You will find another circle when you reach your final home:
That's the faithful, standing hand in hand, around the Father's throne.
Every daughter will be cherished, no son left to weep alone,
in the loving family circle of the souls God calls his own.

Themes/occasions: Love for neighbor. Forgiveness. Family. All Saints Day.
Acceptance of others. Father God. Heaven. Community of faith. Social conflict.

Scripture suggestions: Ephesians 3:14–17. Ephesians 4:1–6. Ephesians 4:31–32.
James 2:1–6. Romans 12:9–18. Galatians 6:1–10. Ecclesiastes 4:9–12.
Mark 12:30. Luke 10:25–37. Acts 2:41–47. 1 John 4:7. Matthew 5:23–24.
Matthew 18:21–22.

Musical settings: BEECHER; CLEANSING FOUNTAIN

53. Family Circle of God (S)

1. Look around your family circle. Are there breaks you ought to mend?
Have old quarrels made you enemies, instead of dearest friends?
Now's the time for you to find an olive branch you can extend.
Let your circle be unbroken once again. *R.*

R. There's one circle won't be broken in days to come, above;
that's the family circle of God.
Join your brothers and your sisters, encircled by his love,
in the everlasting family of God!

2. Look around your inner circle. Do the people you hold dear
know how much you really love them? Have you made that message
   clear?
Share their sorrows and their joys. Confess your burdens and your fears.
Then you'll bind your circle closer through the years. *R.*

3. Look around your widest circle. Does a biased pattern show?
Are the "different" folks not good enough for you to want to know?
Open up your heart and love them. Let your preconceptions go,
and you'll see how big your circle then can grow! *R.*

4. You will find another circle when you reach your final home:
That's the faithful, standing hand in hand, around the Father's throne.
Every daughter will be cherished, no son left to weep alone,
in the family of souls he calls his own! *R.*

Themes/occasions: Love for neighbor. Forgiveness. Family. All Saints Day.
Acceptance of others. Father God. Heaven. Community of faith. Social conflict.
Scripture suggestions: Ephesians 3:14–17. Ephesians 4:1–6. Ephesians 4:31–32.
James 2:1–6. Romans 12:9–18. Galatians 6:1–10. Ecclesiastes 4:9–12.
Mark 12:30. Luke 10:25–37. Acts 2:41–47. 1 John 4:7. Matthew 5:23–24.
Matthew 18:21–22.
Musical setting: SALVATIONIST, alt.

54. Go, and Tell the World

1. Tell people, one by one,
what Jesus Christ has done.
In time, you'll tell the world!
The moment that you spend
might save your dearest friend.
So, go, and tell the world!

2. When you knock on a door,
tell your truth, nothing more.
That's how you tell the world!
Your witness will ring true
if it comes straight from you.
Oh, go, and tell the world!

3. Through sharing, not debate,
in Christian love, not hate,
set out to tell the world!
Then follow, as you pray,
the Holy Spirit's way,
and go, and tell the world!

4. You needn't rouse a crowd
by preaching long and loud
to try to tell the world!
A whisper or a shout
can get God's message out
to go and tell the world!

5. The gospel may be heard
without a single word.
Your faith will tell the world!
Your life is all it takes
to show the change He makes.
Now, go! And tell the world!

Themes/occasions: Christian witness. Evangelism. Ministry and outreach.
Holy Spirit. Truth.
Scripture suggestions: Mark 16:15. 2 Corinthians 4:1–15. 1 Corinthians 2:1–5.
Titus 3:9. 1 Peter 3:15–16. Matthew 5:13–16. Matthew 28:19–20. Acts 1:8.
2 Timothy 2:24–26. Habakkuk 2:2–3.
Musical setting: LAUDES DOMINI, alt.

55.   Jesus Walks on City Streets

1. Jesus walks on city streets.
Every person that I meet
could be Jesus' hands and feet,
speak his words of comfort sweet.
As I make my busy way
through the bustling crowd each day,
if I search with eyes of grace,
I find Jesus in each face.

2. Jesus walks amid the throng.
Rich and homeless, weak and strong,
proud and humble, right and wrong
—all to Jesus Christ belong;
every shape and age and hue,
members of his family too.
Treating them as he would do,
I see Jesus' smile shine through.

3. Jesus walks where few will go,
with the ones few want to know,
love and kindness quick to show
for the lowest of the low.
Lonely corners in the night
suddenly glow neon bright
if, like Jesus, I invite
all to walk within his light.

4. Jesus walks in open air,
through the parks and city square.
He may sit for hours there,
taking time for rest and prayer.
In the town, I too can find
quiet space to fill my mind
with a synergy divine:
God and city intertwined.

Themes/occasions: Love for neighbor. Acceptance of others. Rest. Ministry and outreach. God's presence. Jesus Christ's ministry and miracles. Invitation. Light. Service. City.

Scripture suggestions: Matthew 25:31–46. Micah 6:8. Mark 1:35. Mark 6:31–32. James 2:1–5. Colossians 3:17. Ephesians 4:32.

Musical setting: MESSIAH, alt.

---

56. Come, Dance with Me

1. Come, dance with me, dear partner Jesus,
and guide my footsteps in wondrous ways.
If I but follow your perfect leading,
a graceful rhythm will rule my days.

2. Come, dance with me, O Holy Spirit!
My heart is bursting with love and joy!
I'll dance like David, with pure abandon,
as glad and free as a strong young boy!

3. Come, dance with me, beloved Abba,
a waltz of glorious elegance.
Upon your arm, I will glide and twirl in
a sacred Father and daughter dance.

4. Come, dance with me, my friends and neighbors!
Join hands and voices in harmony.
If all the world moved to God's sweet music,
how grand and peaceful life's dance would be!

Themes/occasions: Father God. Praise. Love for God. Love for neighbor. Music. Holy Spirit. David. God's presence. Father's Day. Unity. Guidance. Trinity.

Scripture suggestions: 2 Samuel 6. Ephesians 5:18–20.

Musical setting: ALMA, alt.

57. Reach Deep into Your Faith

1. Reach deep, reach deep into your faith, and show it to the world.
Raise high the flag of Jesus Christ, and let it fly unfurled.
Tell everyone what he has done, the blood he shed for you.
Reach deep, reach deep into your faith. Help others find faith too.

2. Reach deep, reach deep into your hope, and share it with the world.
Tell every man and woman, teach every boy and girl
that Jesus waits at heaven's gates to welcome them as friends.
Reach deep, reach deep into your hope of life that never ends.

3. Reach deep, reach deep into your love, and pray this for the world:
that enemies may soon join hands, their warring fists uncurled.
Though never can we understand the peace Christ came to give,
reach deep, reach deep into your love for peaceful ways to live.

4. Reach deep, reach deep into your joy, and sing to all the world
how Jesus held you in his arms when trouble 'round you swirled,
how he draws near with words of cheer to bless you on your way.
Reach deep, reach deep into your joy. Proclaim it every day!

Themes/occasions: Evangelism. Christian witness. Redemption. Heaven.
Eternal life. Peace. God's presence. Love for neighbor. Social conflict. Faith.
Love. Hope. Salvation.

Scripture suggestions: Habakkuk 2:2–3. John 3:16–18. Philippians 4:7.
Mark 16:15. Acts 1:8. 1 Corinthians 2:1–5. 2 Corinthians 4:1–15. 1 John 2:1–2.
1 Peter 3:15–16. Matthew 5:13–16. Matthew 28:19–20. 2 Timothy 2:24–26.
Romans 5:1–11. Ephesians 3:14–21.

Musical setting: ELLACOMBE

58. Your Road to Heaven

1. Will your road to heaven lead you far from your native land,
living the great commission wherever God may command?
Will you surrender your comforts to preach from God's Holy Word
on distant soil where the gospel has never yet been heard?
Or by a hint of hardship will you soon be deterred? *R.*

R. Do good while on the journey for which God gave you birth,
for you're on your road to heaven right now, right here on earth.

2. Will your road to heaven keep you close to where you began,
there to befriend the orphan, the widow, the lonely man?
If failing health should confine you to home or bed or a chair,
will you serve God as you're able, by offering love and prayer,
or spend your days bemoaning the cross that you must bear? *R.*

3. Will your road to heaven lead you to some exalted place?
Will you view wealth and power as instruments of God's grace
and use your lofty position "for just a time such as this,"
to advocate for the helpless whom favored folk dismiss?
Or will you shrug when justice gives way to avarice? *R.*

4. Will your road to heaven lead you through the mean streets of town,
into the slums and prisons, where souls have been beaten down?
Will you pass by them, declaring, "From sin their troubles were hewn,"
as if from sin and misfortune you somehow were immune?
Or will you stop and gently bind up your neighbor's wound? *R.*

5. Will your road to heaven lead you to your last stop alone?
When you encounter lost ones who can't make it on their own,
will you help carry their burdens and your provisions divide?
To reach your shared destination, will you serve as their guide?
Or in your haste for heaven, will you push them aside? *R.*

Themes/occasions: Love for neighbor. The Great Commission. Justice. Prayer.
Service. Social conflict. Sanctity of life. Ministry and outreach.

Scripture suggestions: Matthew 25:31–46. Luke 10:25–37. Luke 16:19–31.
Micah 6:8. Galatians 6:2–3. Galatians 6:8–10. Esther 4:6–17. Isaiah 58.

Musical setting: SPARROW, alt.

59. Lift Up Your Voice

1. Lift up your voice in prayer and praise!
To Christ a hymn of celebration raise.
All voices join in harmony and pow'r
to thank him everywhere and every hour.

2. Lift up your eyes to Jesus' face!
Of condemnation, you will see no trace.
Our savior's eyes, so kind and gentle, shine
upon each penitent, with love divine.

3. Lift up your heart! Draw strength and grace
from Christ to run your God-appointed race.
Let fresh, new life your fainting heart inflood,
as you receive his body and his blood.

4. Lift up your ears! The truth embrace!
To holy scripture give a central place.
The spirit fills the open ear that seeks
the living, active Word, through which God speaks.

5. Lift up your hands! Devote your days
to putting faith to work in selfless ways.
Keep Jesus' love in all you say and do,
and he'll produce abundant fruit in you.

Themes/occasions: Praise. The Bible. Forgiveness. Holy Communion. Service. Discipleship. Truth. Ministry and outreach.

Scripture suggestions: 2 Timothy 3:14–17. 2 Timothy 4:1–8. Hebrews 12:1–4. Philippians 3:13–14. Psalm 19:7–8. John 3:16–17. Ephesians 3:14–21. John 15:1–8. Isaiah 40:28–31. James 2:14–17.

Musical setting: TRURO

60. Maybe Yes and Maybe No

1. God, I know you're always there
when I come to you in prayer.
But it's still a mystery:
What's your answer going to be?
Oftentimes you answer, "Yes,"
kindly granting my request.
Oh, the joy and peace it brings
to have your blessing in those things!

2. Other times you tell me, "No,
that is not the way to go."
You are wise enough to see
danger waiting there for me.
Maybe yes and maybe no.
What more do I need to know?
I will trust you, either way,
to love and guide me every day.

Themes/occasions: Prayer. God's will. Trust. Faith. Guidance. God's presence.
Scripture suggestions: Philippians 4:6–7. Psalm 116:1–2. Luke 22:39–46.
Matthew 26:36–56. Mark 14:32–42. Isaiah 30:20–21. Jeremiah 29:11–13.
Musical setting: MARTYN, alt.

61. Don't Be Afraid

1. Don't be afraid. The things you think are impossible,
the Lord can do. Put your trust in him.
Don't be afraid. The Holy Spirit makes possible
God's will for you. Put your trust in him.

2. One day you hear the call of God to a strange new place.
The great unknown fills your heart with dread.
But be assured, the Lord will guide you along the way
and give you grace for the work ahead.

3. When life is harsh and you feel trapped in an endless maze,
don't let despair suffocate your soul.
Have faith in God, who uses even our darkest days
for his good plans. He is in control.

4. When death draws near, the Lord of love will draw nearer still
and hold you close till your life shall cease.
Yes, even then, take comfort knowing his gracious will:
new life with him, one of joy and peace.

5. Don't be afraid. The things you think are impossible,
the Lord can do. Put your trust in him.
Don't be afraid. The Holy Spirit makes possible
God's will for you. Put your trust in him.

Themes/occasions: God's plan. Faith. Invitation. Holy Spirit. Death and dying.
Adversity. Trust. God's power and protection. God's presence. Guidance.
Comfort. God's love. God's will.

Scripture suggestions: Genesis 12:1–4. Jeremiah 1:4–8. Luke 1:30–37.
1 Thessalonians 5:24. Philippians 4:13. Isaiah 41:9–13. Ephesians 3:14–21.
Acts 1:8.

Musical setting: POSSIBLE

62.   In the Armor of God

1. We must be prepared to enter a holy war,
for we'll soon find the enemy at our front door.
But the war against injustice and hate and sin
is a war believers can surely win. *R.*

R. We're more than conquerors, more than victors,
in the armor of God.
Who can stand against us when we stand protected
in the armor of God?

2. Let the belt of truth be buckled around your waist
and the breastplate of righteousness securely placed.
Hold the shield of faith before you, and raise the sword
of the Spirit, found in God's holy Word. *R.*

3. Don the helmet of salvation, and fit your feet
with the gospel of peace to be prepared and fleet.
Now complete your suit of armor by taking care
to surround yourself with a cloak of prayer. *R.*

Themes/occasions: Spiritual warfare. God's power and protection. Faith.
God's presence. Salvation. Social conflict. Justice.
Scripture suggestions: Ephesians 6:11–17. Romans 8:37. 1 Peter 5:8.
Isaiah 41:9–13. Psalm 144. Psalm 3. Romans 12:21. 1 John 4:4–6.
2 Samuel 22. Deuteronomy 20:1–4. 1 Peter 4.
Musical setting: ARMOR OF GOD, alt.

63. When Anguished Cries Are Our Only Word

1. When anguished cries are our only word
and sighs our only song,
our every sorrowful sound is heard
by Him to whom we belong.

2. When pleading hands are our only prayer,
our souls can rest assured,
we need no language but this to share
our deepest hurt with the Lord.

3. When groans of pain are our only speech
and on our knees we fall,
our brokenness does not fail to reach
the heart that understands all.

4. When labored breaths are our only voice,
when even whispers cease,
with silent psalms let us yet rejoice
in God's great mercy and peace.

Themes/occasions: Prayer. Adversity. Death and dying. God's love. Peace.
God's presence. Comfort. Loss. Mourning. Mental illness.

Scripture suggestions: Psalm 55:17–18. Psalm 88:1–3. Psalm 116:1–2.
Habakkuk 3:17–19. Exodus 4:31. Romans 5:2–5. Romans 8:26–27.

Musical setting: LAND OF REST/Sweet Land of Rest

64. Lord, Life Has Laid Us Low

1. Lord, life has laid us low,
blow after crushing blow.
Weak and defenseless, we call your name.
Stretch forth your mighty hand.
Send forth the angel band,
your saving power to proclaim!

2. Jesus, your promised birth
brought peace to all the earth,
yet, sometimes peace seems so hard to find!
O heaven's holy son,
bring hope to everyone
and peace to every troubled mind.

3. Lord, when we can't go on,
mourning for loved ones gone,
take loneliness and despair away.
Jesus, O best of friends,
hold us till grieving ends
and we can see a brighter day.

4. Lord, we are sore and tired,
in work and worry mired,
burdened by so many tasks to do.
Come, place your lighter yoke
on heavy-laden folk,
and help us find our rest in you.

Themes/occasions: Adversity. Mourning. Rest. Loss. Peace. Blue Christmas.
Christmas. God's presence. Mental illness.

Scripture suggestions: Revelation 21:1–4. 1 Corinthians 12:31. Exodus 4:31.
Habakkuk 3:17–19. Luke 2:14. Daniel 10:19. Matthew 5:4. Matthew 11:28–30.

Musical setting: ST. ELIZABETH

65. Lord, Though I Travel Afar

1. Lord, though I travel afar,
where I go you already are.
I'm not alone!
In every strange new place,
upheld by faith and grace,
I shall find strength to face
any unknown.

2. Lord, as I sail stormy seas,
your presence sets my soul at ease.
I can be brave!
With my almighty guide
always close by my side,
why should I trembling hide
from wind and wave?

3. Lord of the turbulent heights,
your pow'r and love surround my flights.
With you I soar
high above everything,
as on an eagle wing.
Filled with your peace, I sing,
fearful no more.

4. Lord, when you call me to roam,
leaving my dearest ones at home,
I trust your care!
Be their most faithful friend,
comfort them and defend
until my travels end.
This is my prayer.

Themes/occasions: Travelers. Military deployment. Ministry and outreach.
Faith. Trust. Guidance. God's power and protection. God's presence. Family.
Scripture suggestions: Luke 1:30–37. Luke 8:22–25. Matthew 28:19–20.
Genesis 12:1–4. Jeremiah 1:4–8. Philippians 4:13. Romans 8:28. Acts 1:8.
Isaiah 40:28–31. Isaiah 41:9–13. Isaiah 43:1–7. 1 Thessalonians 5:24.
Psalm 107:29–30. Psalm 139:7–12. Daniel 10:19. Ephesians 3:14–21.
2 Corinthians 5:16–18.
Musical setting: ITALIAN HYMN

66. I'm Facing a Giant

1. I'm facing a giant called Fear,
just as David faced fierce Goliath.
How my enemy
towers over me!
I'm too small to defy it.
But I'm armed with love
for the Lord above,
and I know he always is near.
Though I stand alone,
just a sling and stone,
this giant shall disappear.

2. I'm facing a giant called Shame,
just as David faced fierce Goliath.
How can I break free
from its tyranny?
I've sinned; I can't deny it.
But I'm armed with love
for the Lord above
and forgiv'n in his holy name.
So when I have thrown
from my sling one stone,
this giant I'll surely tame.

3. I'm facing a giant called Gloom,
just as David faced fierce Goliath.
Forces I can't see
turn my energy
to dark and deathly quiet.
But I'm armed with love
for the Lord above,
who has called me forth from my tomb.
In his hands, my own
little sling and stone
are sealing this giant's doom.

4. I'm facing a giant called Hate,
just as David faced fierce Goliath.
Greed and bigotry
breed hostility;
old quarrels multiply it.
But I'm armed with love
for the Lord above,
and his reign of peace I await.
When the moss has grown
on my sling and stone,
this giant I'll dominate.

5. I face, on my soul's battlefield,
giants mightier than Goliath.
But my victory
is a certainty,
for my Lord shall supply it.
Yes, I'm armed with love
for the Lord above.
He has been my sword and my shield.
And the pow'r he's shown
through my sling and stone
makes every fierce giant yield.

Themes/occasions: David. Adversity. Hope. Faith. God's presence. Peace.
God's power and protection. Social conflict. Spiritual warfare. Forgiveness.
Mental illness.

Scripture suggestions: 1 Samuel 17. 2 Samuel 22. Deuteronomy 31:8.
Psalm 3. Psalm 40:1–3. Psalm 144. 1 John 4:4–6. 1 John 5:1–5. Exodus 15.
Philippians 4:13. Romans 12:21. Revelation 12:10. Isaiah 41:9–13.

Musical setting: GARDEN

67. O Lord, Please Walk Me Home

1. O Lord, please walk me home,
wherever on earth I roam.
I can't face alone
a future unknown.
O Lord, please walk me home.

2. O Lord, please hold my hand
till I reach the Promised Land.
Stand with me before
that heavenly door.
O Lord, please hold my hand.

3. O Lord, please call my name
and tell me you're glad I came.
Forgive me my sin,
and lead me right in.
O Lord, please call my name.

Themes/occasions: Death and dying. God's presence. Heaven. Eternal life.
Forgiveness.
Scripture suggestions: Psalm 31:1–5. Psalm 37:23–25. Luke 19:10.
Musical setting: DENNIS

68. Sweet, Sweet Fragrance of Love

1. A woman once anointed Jesus' feet with precious nard.
She wiped them with her hair, as fragrance bloomed from one small jar.
And her act of love spread pleasing perfume
far and wide, to heaven above,
filling up that house, yes, every last room,
with a scent that Jesus breathed deeply of,
with the sweet, sweet fragrance of love.

2. The church, as Jesus' body, honors him by doing the same
when we pour lavish love on one another in his name.
May our acts of love spread pleasing perfume
far and wide, to heaven above,
filling up God's house, yes, every last room,
with a scent that we will breathe deeply of,
with the sweet, sweet fragrance of love.

3. Now Jesus sends us out to share his love with those in need,
to pour the precious balm of gracious word and selfless deed.
May our acts of love spread pleasing perfume
far and wide, to heaven above,
filling up the world, yes, every last room,
with a scent that all can breathe deeply of,
with the sweet, sweet fragrance of love.

Themes/occasions: Love for neighbor. Community of faith. Ministry and outreach.

Scripture suggestions: Luke 7:36–50. Matthew 26:6–13. Galatians 6:9–10.
2 Corinthians 2:14–17. Mark 14:3–9. John 12:1–8.

Musical setting: GRACE WAS ALL THEIR SONG

69.   Wedding Song

1. You know my heart has been wounded before.
How hard it is to trust once more!
But I'll step with you through that open door.
Yes, I will offer you love, my love.

2. I know that humans by God were designed
to learn and grow, new truths to find.
As I change, I'll never leave you behind!
No, I'll grow closer to love, your love.

3. We know the sacrifice married life takes:
to choose what's best for both our sakes,
celebrate success and forgive mistakes,
remaining faithful in love, our love.

4. God knows his plan for all husbands and wives:
a peaceful home where each one thrives.
We will thank and honor him all our lives.
God bless our union with love, his love!

Themes/occasions: Weddings. Love. God's love.
Scripture suggestions: 1 Corinthians 13:4–13. Song of Solomon 4:10.
Ephesians 4:1–6. Ephesians 5:21–33. Genesis 2:18–24. Ecclesiastes 4:9–12.
Musical setting: WOODWORTH

70. Lord, Would You Part the Sea

1. Lord, would you part the sea for me,
halt my pursuing enemy,
lead me out of my slavery?
Lord, would you part the sea for me?

2. Lord, would you cast my demons out,
hush voices in my head that shout,
tormenting me with fear and doubt?
Lord, would you cast my demons out?

3. Lord, would you call me from my grave,
show doubters life you truly gave
when you arrived too late to save?
Lord, would you call me from my grave?

4. Lord, would your hand keep me afloat
if I stepped from a wave-tossed boat
weighed down by doubting's heavy coat?
Lord, would your hand keep me afloat?

5. Lord, would you sweetly speak my name,
set my despairing heart aflame,
if to the garden tomb I came?
Lord, would you sweetly speak my name?

Themes/occasions: God's power and protection. God's presence. God's love.
Scripture suggestions: Exodus 14. Hebrews 11:29. Deuteronomy 7:7–8.
Matthew 8:28–34. Matthew 14:22–36. Mark 1:21–34. Mark 16:1–19.
Luke 8:1–3. John 11:38–44. John 20:11–18. Ephesians 3:14–21.
Musical setting: OLD 100th, alt.

71.   O Dreamer of Dreams

1. O dreamer of dreams from the all-seeing Lord,
know that one day your faith will receive its reward.
Believe in the dreams granted only to you,
for the Lord has the power to make them come true.

2. O dreamer, be patient! O dreamer, be brave!
Choose to trust, not despair, though you serve as a slave.
You languish in chains, but one day you'll be freed
to continue the journey the Lord has decreed.

3. O dreamer, forgive those who once did you wrong.
Their betrayals were part of God's plan all along.
One day, you will see it has all been fulfilled,
and your dreams from the Lord have come true, as he willed.

Themes/occasions: Dreams. God's plan. Waiting. Forgiveness. Trust. Faith.
God's promises. Freedom. Joseph (son of Jacob).
Scripture suggestions: Genesis 37 and 39–45.
Musical setting: FOUNDATION

This page is left blank in order to display the following songs on facing pages. Feel free to scribble notes here.

72. I Wonder, Do Angels Still March

1. I wonder, do angels still march forth from heaven
in legions to battle our enemy,
as God once defended the prophet Elisha
with armies Elisha alone could see?

2. I wonder, do angels still carry from heaven
God's answers to questions from faithful men,
as Gabriel replied to the prayers of Daniel
for exile in Babylon soon to end?

3. I wonder, do angels still come down from heaven,
delivering glad tidings from the Lord,
as Gabriel appeared to the young virgin Mary,
announcing that she would be blessed by God?

4. I wonder, do angels still sing up in heaven,
the skies resonate with their joyful sound,
as choirs rejoiced at the birth of the savior
and praises rang out when the lost was found?

5. I wonder, do angels still hasten from heaven
to strengthen and cheer souls in agony,
as angels gave comfort and courage to Jesus
in his time of trial at Gethsemane?

6. O Lord, send your angels today down from heaven
to serve you on earth as they do above;
and help me to see among faces around me
these mystical ministers of your love.

Themes/occasions: Angels. The Annunciation. Christmas. Prayer. God's power and protection. Comfort. Elisha. Daniel. Mary (mother of Jesus).

Scripture suggestions: 2 Kings 6:8–23. Daniel 9:1–27. Luke 1:5–25. Luke 1:26–38. Luke 2:6–20.Luke 15:3–10. Luke 22:39–46. Hebrews 1:6–7. Hebrews 1:13–14. Matthew 4:1–11. Matthew 26:36–56. Genesis 16:1–16. Revelation 19:9–10. Psalm 91:9–12.

Musical setting: ST. CLEMENT

73. I Wonder, Do Angels Still Sing

1. I wonder, do angels still sing up in heaven,
the skies resonate with their joyful sound,
as choirs rejoiced at the birth of the savior
and praises rang out when the lost was found?

2. I wonder, do angels still come down from heaven,
delivering glad tidings from the Lord,
as Gabriel appeared to the young virgin Mary,
announcing that she would be blessed by God?

3. I wonder, do angels still carry from heaven
the Lord's reassurance to faithful men,
as angels told Joseph in dreams, "Do not worry,
for Mary conceived by God's providence"?

4. I wonder, do angels still hasten from heaven
to guard and protect from an enemy,
as angels warned Joseph of plans to harm Jesus
and told him to rise, take the child, and flee?

5. O Lord, send your angels today down from heaven
to serve you on earth as they do above;
and help me to see in my dreams and my waking
these mystical ministers of your love!

Themes/occasions: Angels. The Annunciation. Christmas. Prayer. Dreams.
God's power and protection. Mary (mother of Jesus). Joseph (father of Jesus).
Scripture suggestions: Luke 1:5–25. Luke 1:26–38. Luke 2:6–20. Luke
15:3–10. Hebrews 1:6–7. Hebrews 1:13–14. Matthew 1:18–25. Matthew
2:13–15. Psalm 91:9–12. Revelation 19:9–10.
Musical setting: ST. CLEMENT

74. Surrounded by the Lord

1. The Lord goes forth in front of me in pillar cloud and fire.
He leads me to the promised land where waits my heart's desire.

2. The Lord is close behind me, too. Upon my Abba's breast
I lay my weary, fretful head for comfort, peace, and rest.

3. The Lord is standing by my side to join my righteous fight.
What enemy can conquer me against his holy might?

4. The Lord is high above my head, inviting me to rise
and soar with him on eagle wings across the lofty skies.

5. The Lord is even under me when I'm dragged down by doubt,
preceding me into the pit, prepared to lift me out.

6. Yes, I'm surrounded by the Lord, whose presence makes me whole,
and ever will his spirit dwell within my heart and soul.

Themes/occasions: God's presence. God's power and protection. Guidance.
God's promises.
Scripture suggestions: Exodus 13:21–22. 1 Samuel 17:32–51. Psalm 3:1–6.
Psalm 16:8. Psalm 40:1–3. Psalm 91. Psalm 139. 2 Timothy 1:14.
Romans 8:11. Romans 8:31–39. Isaiah 40:28–31. Isaiah 41:10–13.
Musical setting: AZMON

75. My Forever Lord

1. Tell me, loving Lord, the promise in your Word:
You, the God who chose to make me,
will not leave me or forsake me.
Tell me once again! I need to be assured.
Though much grief or pain I suffer,
though I'm injured by another,
you will never leave me orphaned and forlorn.
You are my forever Lord.

2. Teach me, holy Lord, the guidance in your Word.
Gently give me your correction
as I strive to reach perfection.
Tell me once again! I'm weak and insecure.
You forgive my past behavior,
and you'll always be my savior;
I will never be abandoned or ignored.
You are my forever Lord.

3. Show, eternal Lord, the comfort in your Word:
flowing through the Bible pages,
steadfast love throughout the ages.
Tell me once again the truth I'm longing for:
Let the world be false and hateful;
you have proven to be faithful.
You will never change. Of that I can be sure.
You are my forever Lord.

Themes/occasions: God's love. God's presence. God's faithfulness. Comfort.
Discipleship. Trust. Adversity. The Bible. Salvation. Forgiveness.
Scripture suggestions: Psalm 66:16–20. Psalm 138. John 8:1–11. John
14:18–19. Matthew 28:18–20. Jeremiah 31:3.
Musical setting: MY FOREVER LORD

76.   Holiness Climbs Great Heights

1. Holiness climbs great heights
when it bows low to serve.
Selfless and humble, it delights
to give without reserve.

2. Holiness does not ask
reasons for God's commands.
Meekly it tackles every task
laid on its heart and hands.

3. Holiness seeks retreat
far from all worldly care,
studying at the Teacher's feet,
refreshed in rest and prayer.

4. Holiness looks beyond
what mortal eyes can see,
finding in faith a sacred bond
with unseen deity.

5. Holiness I (we) aspire
in some small way to gain.
Spur, Holy Spirit, my (our) desire
to greater heights attain.

(Maundy Thursday)   6. Holiness we desire
in some small way to gain.
Kneeling with Jesus, we aspire
to greater heights attain.

Themes/occasions: Maundy Thursday. Holiness. Service. Rest. Humility.
Holy Spirit. Discipleship. Obedience. God's commands.

Scripture suggestions: John 13:14–17. Mark 9:35. Mark 10:43–45.
Philippians 2:3. Isaiah 55:8–9. 1 Peter 1:15–16. Galatians 2:10. Luke 5:15–16.
Luke 10:38–42. Luke 14:11.

Musical setting: TRENTHAM

77.   Lord, Set Fire to My Soul

1. Lord, set fire to my soul!
Burn all trace of sin away.
Touch my lips with searing coal,
worthier your words to say. *R.*

R. Sanctify me, Lord, I pray!
Pure and holy help me stay.

2. Cleansing floods pour on my heart!
Wash all stain of sin away.
Scrub and polish every part.
There your shining love display. *R.*

3. Winds of grace sweep through my mind!
Drive all thought of sin away.
To temptation make me blind
so I'll not be led astray. *R.*

4. On my body, wield your knife!
Cut all cause of sin away.
Take, O Lord, my very life
if it would your love betray. *R.*

Themes/occasions: Holiness. Sin. Grace. Temptation.
Scripture suggestions: Isaiah 6:1–8. Mark 9:43–48. Matthew 5:29–30.
Matthew 6:9–13. Titus 3:3–7. 1 Thessalonians 4:1–8. Romans 7:14–25.
Psalm 51:1–12. Jude 1:17–21.
Musical setting: DIX

78. Peering into Faith's Foggy Window

1. Peering into faith's foggy window,
wond'ring if a God does exist ...
Would he see my questions as ego?
Damn me for these doubts that persist?
Till I see a sign,
I can't make up my mind.
Could there be some proof that I missed?

2. Knocking on the door to salvation,
wond'ring, Is it mine to receive?
Jesus says he offers redemption
free to all who hear and believe.
Is this precious grace
a gift I should embrace?
Or a promise made to deceive?

3. Staring at my face in the mirror,
wond'ring how the years slipped away ...
Thoughts of life in some far hereafter
plague me, but I hold them at bay.
Searching for "the truth"
was just a whim of youth.
I've more urgent business today.

4. Gazing at the gateway to heaven,
wond'ring what it looks like inside ...
Are there streets of gold and a mansion
peopled with my dear ones who've died?
Will I ever know?
Is heaven where I'll go?
How much time is left to decide?

5. Pondering my life's final chapter,
looking back at choices I made ...
Now I see not questions, but answers,
know the joy it cost me to wait.
Lost, because I'd been
still outside, peering in
through the foggy window of faith.

Themes/occasions: Faith. Questioning. Death and dying. Eternal life. Heaven.
Grace. Redemption. Salvation. Truth.

Scripture suggestions: Revelation 21:10–21. Romans 1:16–21. Psalm 53.
Proverbs 1:20–33. 1 John 2:1–2. John 20:24–31. Hebrews 4:1–7.

Musical setting: PICARDY

79. O Lord, I Look Back on My Life

1. O Lord, I look back on my life
and find, through sorrow and through strife,
your constant presence by my side;
yes, while your very being I've
so stubbornly denied.

2. O Lord, I see your kindness shine
in blessings born of your design.
"All things together work for good."
If only I had claimed as mine
the promise that they would!

3. O Lord, you loved me even when
I gloried in my sin. But then,
with voice too tender to ignore,
you spoke my name and called me gently,
"Come, and sin no more."

4. O Lord, my failings I confess,
my faith and grateful love profess.
You raise me from my knees and say,
"Now walk with me in humbleness,
and learn to love my way."

5. O Lord, I weep for shame, aghast,
to clearly see my sin at last.
Though you forgive, I've caused you pain
and hurt so many in the past
whose grievous wounds remain.

6. O Lord, my deeds I can't erase.
Their consequences I must face.
But hope soars high above regret,
and your redeeming love and grace
will lift me higher yet!

Themes/occasions: Funerals and memorials. Church milestones.
Remembrance. Grace. Hope. Redemption. Penitence. God's love. God's
presence. Forgiveness.
Scripture suggestions: Psalm 66:16–20. Psalm 103. Micah 6:8. Romans 5:1–11.
Romans 8:1–12. Romans 8:28. John 8:2–11. 1 John 4:9–10. Luke 19:10.
Jude 1:17–25.
Musical setting: ST. MARGARET

80. Pray for Me, O Holy Spirit

1. Pray for me, O Holy Spirit! Pray in sighs too deep for words!
At God's throne, your fervent groaning, though unspoken, shall be heard.
I don't know what I should hope for, how to pray the way I ought.
See my need; with constant pleading, pray for me when I cannot.

2. Pray for us, that we may thus retain an advocate on high.
On our knees with guilty pleas, on your good counsel we rely.
May for us the seat of justice now the seat of mercy be!
Oh, implore the righteous Lord to judge our souls with clemency!

3. Pray for all who humbly call upon the name of Jesus Christ;
and for those who don't yet know him, let your earnest prayers rise.
How can any mortal man refute the Holy Spirit's proof?
Open wide the doubting eye, that all may see your saving truth!

4. Help us pray, both night and day, for one another without cease.
Lend your ear, for you can hear our neighbor's secret cares and needs.
Even though we may not know what words of prayer for each are best,
Spirit, cry to God on high for those on whom our prayers rest.

Themes/occasions: Prayer. Holy Spirit. Forgiveness. Truth. Love for neighbor.
Judgment.
Scripture suggestions: Romans 1:16–21. Romans 8:26–27. 1 John 2:1–2.
John 16:7–15. 2 Timothy 4:1–8. 1 Thessalonians 5:12–24. Ephesians 6:17–20.
Jude 1:17–25.
Musical setting: NETTLETON

81.   Teach Me Truth, O Holy Spirit

1. Teach me truth, O Holy Spirit! Help my finite mind to span
God's decree:
the Christ would be
the Son of God, yet Son of Man.
Holy Spirit! Holy Spirit! Grant a glimpse of heaven's plan.

2. Bare my soul, O Holy Spirit! Lay my sins down at my door.
I, confessing,
seek his blessing:
"Go in peace, and sin no more."
Holy Spirit! Holy Spirit! Cleanse me to my very core.

3. Pray for me, O Holy Spirit, for my foolish heart knows not
what to pray for,
what to say, or
how to praise God as I ought.
Holy Spirit! Holy Spirit! Speak for me to holy God.

4. Guide my feet, O Holy Spirit! Lead me in God's chosen way.
Keep me going
strong and growing
near to heaven day by day.
Holy Spirit! Holy Spirit! Never let me go astray.

Themes/occasions: Holy Spirit. Guidance. Truth. Discipleship. Penitence.
Scripture suggestions: John 14:15–17. John 14:26. John 16:7–15. Acts 11:12.
Romans 8:1–27. Titus 3:3–7. Luke 12:11–12. Matthew 10:19–20.
Galatians 5:16–26. Jude 1:17–25.
Musical setting: REGENT SQUARE

82. Unseen But Real

1. As the wind freely blows,
so the Lord's Spirit flows.
Its invisible power we feel.
And though no mortal knows
whence it comes, where it goes,
like the wind, the Lord's Spirit is real. *R.*

R. Unseen but real, holy presence we feel
in the touch of the Spirit, who is unseen but real.

2. As the human eye sees
how the wind sways the trees,
so the Spirit's true nature is shown:
Sinners fall to their knees;
the despairing find peace.
By its work, the Lord's Spirit is known. *R.*

3. Like a breeze's light brush
or a tempest's wild rush,
the Lord's Spirit moves in its own way,
from a comforting hush
'mid the world's noisy crush
to a whirlwind that blows doubts away. *R.*

Themes/occasions: Holy Spirit. Faith. God's presence. Peace. God's power.
Penitence.

Scripture suggestions: John 3:5–8. John 14:15–17. John 14:26. John 16:7–15.
Titus 3:3–7. Romans 8:1–27. Galatians 5:16–26.

Musical setting: TRUST AND OBEY

This page is left blank in order to display the following songs on facing pages. Feel free to scribble notes here.

83. The Road to Heav'n

1. The road to heav'n looked long and rough.
The road I chose instead
was short and smooth, and soon enough
I learned where that road led:
a fast, reckless ride, a slippery slide,
a headlong tumble from grace.
And now I hide for shame inside
a godforsaken place.

2. A still, small voice says, "Child, you're wrong.
I've not forsaken you.
Come back to me, where you belong.
My home is your home too."
My sad head I bow, for I don't know how
to climb a mountain so high.
I say, "For me it's too late now,
too hard to even try."

3. A new voice says, "It's not too late.
Believe, and you will see.
I am the Way to heaven's gate.
Come now, and follow me."
Before me He stands with two outstretched hands
that bear the marking of nails.
I reach, but, bound by sin's strong bands,
my burst of courage fails.

4. A third voice says, "The debt you owed
was paid to set you free.
I'll help you on the upward road.
Come, live eternally."
The pit once so deep, the hill once so steep
can hold me captive no more.
God's love was always mine to keep!
On wings of grace I soar!

Themes/occasions: Redemption. Holy Spirit. Trinity. Grace. Forgiveness. Sin.
God's love. Temptation. Faith.
Scripture suggestions: Romans 5:6–11. Romans 8:1–17. Romans 8:31–39.
John 3:16–17. John 14:1–6. Matthew 7:13–15. 1 John 2:1–2. 1 John 5:1–5.
1 John 4:12–18. Luke 15:11–24. Luke 23:39–43. Ephesians 1:4–10.
Ephesians 2:1–10. Ephesians 3:14–21. Jude 1:17–21. Titus 3:3–7.
Musical setting: THIS ENDRIS NYGHT

84. Thy Will Be Done

1. When I recite the words that Jesus taught us,
"Thy kingdom come; thy will be done," I pray.
But in my mind, these words are lightly spoken;
I don't sincerely wish for what I say.
I hesitate to put myself in your hands,
to truly hope your will is done today.

2. You see, I've heard believers tell each other
that grief and agony must be our lot.
"It is God's will," they say when people suffer.
"Resign yourself to God's will," they have taught.
But if it brings us only pain and sorrow,
how can I pray for your will as I ought?

3. Your Holy Spirit draws me to the Bible.
For your assurance, that's the place to look.
Your loving will was long ago inscribed there,
upon the pages of your sacred book.
I read that earthly trials are temporary.
Your will for me is pleasing, perfect, good.

4. This is God's will: that I, though undeserving,
shall be the heir to heaven through his son.
Because Christ died, I shall inherit glory,
eternal life, when this world's race is run.
What lavish grace! I joyfully surrender!
With all my soul, I pray, "Thy will be done!"

Themes/occasions: God's will. Trust. The Bible. Eternal life. Adversity. Holy Spirit. Prayer.

Scripture suggestions: Romans 12:2. Matthew 6:9–10. 1 Peter 1:3–9. Ephesians 1:4–10. Ephesians 3:14–21. John 6:40.

Musical settings: FINLANDIA; THY WILL BE DONE

85. Not Our Way but Yours, O Lord

R. Not our way but yours, O Lord, the way that's right and sure.
You shall be the way, the truth, the life forevermore.

1. You gave a great commission, equipped and sent us forth.
But when you said, "Go south now," instead we headed north. *R.*

2. You called us back, reminding that your way was the best.
But when you said, "Go east now," instead we headed west. *R.*

3. You marked our route with arrows so there would be no doubt.
But when you said, "Go in now," instead we headed out. *R.*

4. You stopped us when we wandered and turned us right around.
But when you said, "Go up now," instead we headed down. *R.*

5. But then we saw how meekly you walked to Calvary.
We listen when you call us, "Come now, and follow me!" *R.*

Themes/occasions: Obedience. God's will. Sovereign Lord. God's commands.
The Great Commission. Guidance. Calvary. Holy Week. Good Friday.
Scripture suggestions: Jonah. Isaiah 30:19–21. Isaiah 48:17–18. Acts 8:20–40.
Philippians 2:8. Matthew 28:16–20. John 19:13–18. Jeremiah 7:23–28.
Musical settings: ROYAL OAK, alt.; ALL THINGS BRIGHT

86. The Hand of God Created Me

1. The hand of God created me
according to a plan
that I, as wise as I may be,
could never understand.
I see a glimpse of holy will
and gratefully obey,
until my hope shall be fulfilled
to live with God someday.

2. The Holy Spirit plunged me in-
to Jordan's cleansing flow
and washed away the stain of sin
from Eden long ago.
It lifted up my shiv'ring soul
and wrapped my nakedness
inside the pure and shining robe
of Jesus' righteousness.

3. The voice of Jesus called me thus
from cold and lonely doom:
He spoke my name, like Lazarus,
"Come forth now from your tomb!"
My sinful nature wants me dead,
but when Christ's name I shout,
he lays his hand upon my head
and casts my demons out.

4. For my appointed time I wait.
When I'm called home at last
and I arrive at heaven's gate,
recalling mercies past,
I shall be unafraid but awed
in sacred presence of
Creator, Spirit, Savior: God,
already known and loved.

Themes/occasions: Creation. Trinity. Salvation. Eternal life. Sin. Lazarus.
Holy Spirit. Heaven. Temptation.

Scripture suggestions: John 11:38–44. John 14. Isaiah 55:8–9. Isaiah 61:10.
Genesis 3. Psalm 51:1–12. Psalm 139:14–16. 1 Corinthians 13:12. 2 Kings
5:1–14. Titus 3:3–7. Matthew 3:1–6. Mark 1:21–34. Mark 16:9. Ephesians
1:4–10. Ephesians 2:5. Luke 8:2.

Musical setting: KINGSFOLD/LAZARUS

87. This Sparrow Has a Broken Wing

1. O God, you keep your loving eye
on every single living thing.
Yes, little sparrows such as I
are cared for by our gracious King.
O you created me to fly
and taught me joyful songs to sing,
but now in pain to you I cry.
This sparrow has a broken wing.

2. You nudged me from my nest one day.
I tried to soar so high and free,
on wings not meant to fly that way.
I fell to earth beneath my tree.
A wounded bird is easy prey,
but in your care I know I'll be.
For even sparrows trust and say,
"My God is watching over me."

3. A hungry fox is on my track.
But you, my God, with loving care
not only save me from attack,
but grant this sparrow's eager prayer.
You swoop and take me on your back
and lift me swiftly through the air.
You'll always be the wings I lack,
the pow'r to fly where eagles dare!

Themes/occasions: God's presence. God's power and protection. Prayer. God's provision. Nature. Creation.

Scripture suggestions: Matthew 6:25–33. Matthew 10:29–31. Luke 12:6–7. Isaiah 40:28–31. Exodus 19:1–4. Psalm 3:1–6. Deuteronomy 32:7–12.

Musical settings: CANDLER/YE BANKS AND BRAES; ST. PATRICK

This page is left blank in order to display the following songs on facing pages. Feel free to scribble notes here.

88. Your Heavens Stretch Before Me (S)

1. Your heavens stretch before me, as I view the nighttime skies.
How boundless is the darkness! How far the starry lights!
Lord God who made the planets, placing each upon its course,
O you have set your glory above the universe. *(R.)*

2. Your sea rolls on beyond me, as across the deep I gaze.
How vast the heaving ocean! How numberless its waves!
Lord God who made the water and the current and the tide,
O you wield power greater than all of nature's might. *(R.)*

3. Your land spreads out below me, as on mountain peak I stand.
How varied are its wonders! How rich, complex, and grand!
Lord God who made its creatures to such intricate design,
O you cannot be fathomed by any mortal mind. *(R.)*

4. (or R.) What, then, are human beings, that you care so much for us?
Amid creation's splendor, but tiny specks of dust!
Yet you have made us rulers of the works your hands have made.
In all the earth, your people adore you and exclaim:
O Lord! O how majestic and holy is your name!

Themes/occasions: Creation. Nature. God's power and protection. Praise.
Sovereign Lord. Psalm songs.
Scripture suggestions: Psalm 8. Hebrews 2. Psalm 19:1–6. Ephesians 3:14–21.
Musical setting: SHENANGO

89. Your Heavens Stretch Before Me (BH)

1. Your heavens stretch before me, as I view the nighttime skies.
How boundless is the darkness! How far the starry lights!
Lord God who made the planets, placing each upon its course,
O you have set your glory above the universe. *R.*

R. What, then, are humans, that you care for us?
'Mid creation's splendor, mere specks of dust!
Yet you appoint us to rule your domain.
O Lord, how majestic is your holy name!

2. Your sea rolls on beyond me, as across the deep I gaze.
How vast the heaving ocean! How numberless its waves!
Lord God who made the water and the current and the tide,
O you wield power greater than all of nature's might. *R.*

3. Your land spreads out below me, as on mountain peak I stand.
How varied are its wonders! How rich, complex, and grand!
Lord God who made its creatures to such intricate design,
O you cannot be fathomed by any mortal mind. *R.*

Themes/occasions: Creation. Nature. God's power and protection. Praise.
Sovereign Lord. Psalm songs.
Scripture suggestions: Psalm 8. Hebrews 2. Psalm 19:1–6. Ephesians 3:14–21.
Musical setting: BEACON HILL, alt.

90. Close My Eyes

Close my eyes. Let worries cease.
Fill my mind with perfect peace.

Free me, for a while, from pain,
that my strength I may regain.

Let sweet slumber come and stay.
Hold me, Lord, till break of day.

Themes/occasions: Evening. Rest. Peace. Adversity. Healing. Comfort.
God's power and protection.

Scripture suggestions: Matthew 11:28. Psalm 3:5. Psalm 4:8. Romans 8:6.
Philippians 4:6–7. John 14:27. Proverbs 3:1, 24.

Musical setting: REDHEAD 76/PETRA

91. O Father God, Dear Abba

1. O Father God, dear Abba, I climb upon your knee
to read the Holy Bible, the book you wrote for me.
I beg for one more story; my head begins to nod.
(A) You hold me close and tell me you love me, Father God.
(B) You hold me close and tell me how you love me, Father God.

2. O Father God, dear Abba, how wonderful you are!
I find you in the stories of people near and far,
from Genesis' beginning to Revelation's end,
(A) our maker and our savior, our everlasting friend.
(B) our maker and our savior and our everlasting friend.

3. O Father God, dear Abba, in every verse I see
how strong and wise and tender a father's love can be.
Within your arms I nestle, eyes fixed upon your face.
(A) You kiss my brow and rock me to sleep in your embrace.
(B) You kiss my brow and rock me till I yield to sleep's embrace.

Themes/occasions: Father God. The Bible. Father's Day. God's presence.
Evening. God's love. God's faithfulness. Baptisms.
Scripture suggestions: Romans 8:14–17. 1 John 3:1. Matthew 6:5–15.
Matthew 7:9–11. Matthew 11:25–27. Hebrews 2:10–12. Ephesians 3:14–21.
Ephesians 6:1–4. Psalm 68:4–6. Jeremiah 31:3. Luke 11:11–13.
Musical settings: AURELIA; BLAIRGOWRIE

92. Resting, Resting

R. Resting, resting,
ceasing our labors to rest and pray.
Resting, resting,
resting with Jesus this Sabbath day.

1. Flow'rs of the field do not toil or spin;
yet by the Lord they're splendidly dressed.
Seek first his kingdom, and trust in him.
Knowing our needs, he'll provide the rest. *R.*

2. Trying too hard more work to complete
makes us, like Martha, fretful of heart.
Quietly sitting at Jesus' feet
chooses, like Mary, the better part. *R.*

Themes/occasions: Rest. Sabbath. God's provision. Sovereign Lord. Nature.
Mary (of Bethany). Martha. Trust.
Scripture suggestions: Matthew 6:25–34. Matthew 11:28–30. Mark 6:31.
Philippians 4:6–7. Luke 5:15–16. Luke 10:38–42. Exodus 20:8–11.
Genesis 2:1–3. Hebrews 4:9–11.
Musical setting: MOODY, alt.

93. Don't Rush Away

1. Don't rush away from the throne of grace.
Jesus, the King, loves you.
Linger, and gaze on his holy face.
Jesus, the King, loves you. *R.*

R. Don't hurry through your prayer.
Why dash away?
Quietly stay.
Savor the time you share.
Jesus, the King, loves you.

2. Look! He has saved you a special place.
Jesus, the King, loves you.
Right at his feet there's a waiting space.
Jesus, the King, loves you. *R.*

3. He longs to hear all about your days.
Jesus, the King, loves you.
Tell him your troubles. Sing songs of praise.
Jesus, the King, loves you. *R.*

4. Halt, for an hour, your hectic pace.
Jesus, the King, loves you.
Slow down and rest in his calm embrace.
Jesus, the King, loves you. *R.*

Themes/occasions: Christ the King. God's love. Rest. God's presence.
Scripture suggestions: Matthew 2:1–2. Matthew 25:31–46. Luke 1:26–33.
John 18:33–37. Ecclesiastes 8:3. Revelation 1:4–8. Jeremiah 23:5–6.
Ephesians 3:14–21.
Musical setting: MARTIN

94. You Know My Heart

1. You know my heart. You know my soul,
my thoughts to you an open scroll.
O Jesus, first and dearest friend,
with you I never need pretend.
My failings freely I confess,
assured that you won't love me less. *R.*

R. No truer love could ever be,
than your forever love for me.

2. You hold my heart. You hold my soul,
my pain to heal, my grief console.
Secure within your strong embrace,
I'm soothed by your restoring grace.
Hold tight, and never let me go!
Still closer I desire to grow. *R.*

3. You lift my heart. You lift my soul
to help me reach my heav'nly goal.
In times of trial, when I'm hard pressed,
you urge me on to meet each test.
With strength and courage drawn from you,
I know there's nothing I can't do. *R.*

4. You are my heart. You are my soul,
and in your love am I made whole,
no longer facing life alone,
since you made me your very own.
We two shall share a lifelong bond,
in life on earth and life beyond. *R.*

Themes/occasions: God's love. God's presence. Comfort. Eternal life.
Scripture suggestions: James 1:3–4. John 3:16. John 15:9–17. Psalm 63:1–8.
Psalm 139:1–16. Psalm 100. 1 John 1:9. 1 John 5:20. Philippians 3:12–14.
Philippians 4:13. Romans 5:3–5. Deuteronomy 6:5. Deuteronomy 7:9.
1 Corinthians 13:13. Ephesians 3:14–21. Zephaniah 3:17.
Musical setting: SWEET HOUR

95. Waiting, Waiting

1. Teach me to wait for your open door,
trust and obey your will for this day.
In my impatience to serve you more,
I rush away when I should just pray. *R.*

R. Waiting, waiting, clinging to faith in God's perfect plans.
Waiting, waiting, leaving my life in the Master's hands.

2. "Woe to those heard saying, 'Let us see
what God will do. Now, make it come true.'"
Those warning words could be meant for me.
I must renew, Lord, my trust in you. *R.*

3. When will temptation and trouble cease?
Lord, how much longer can I stay strong?
Flood every part of me with your peace.
Help me hold on for your victory song. *R.*

4. Quiet my questions and calm my mind.
Soon enough, I will know how and why.
But if those answers aren't mine to find,
I still rely on you, God Most High. *R.*

Themes/occasions: Trust. Faith. God's plan. God's will. Questioning.
Discipleship. Temptation. Sovereign Lord.

Scripture suggestions: Isaiah 5:18–19. Habakkuk 2:1–3. Psalm 27:14.
Psalm 62:1–2. Job 38–42. Isaiah 40:28–31. Isaiah 55:6–11. Proverbs 3:5–6.
Ephesians 1:9–10. Ephesians 3:14–21. Ephesians 6:18. Jeremiah 29:11–13.
1 Corinthians 13:12. 1 John 5:1–5.

Musical setting: MOODY

96.   Thus Far the Lord Has Helped Me

1. When trials begin and doubt creeps in,
when joy is turned to sorrow,
then come what may, I'll stand and say,
"I shall not fear tomorrow!"
I'll rest assured and trust the Lord,
for safe he's always kept me.
The proof is cast in my own past:
Thus far the Lord has helped me!

2. As Samuel, God's praise to tell,
the Stone of Help erected,
I'll raise my cry to testify:
"See how I've been protected!"
Though some who hear resent or sneer
at blessings God has dealt me,
this truth can't hide or be denied:
Thus far the Lord has helped me!

3. I can't explain why mortal pain
God's son endured to save me.
A wayward child now reconciled,
I marvel, "He forgave me!"
This gracious love from God above,
all undeserved, indwelt me.
Of wondrous things my spirit sings:
"Thus far the Lord has helped me!"

Themes/occasions: God's provision. God's power and protection. Salvation.
God's faithfulness. Adversity. Remembrance. Christian witness. Samuel.
God's love.

Scripture suggestions: 1 Samuel 7:10–12. Psalm 3:1–6. Psalm 22.
Psalm 46:1–7. Habakkuk 3:17–19.

Musical setting: ENDLESS SONG, alt.

97. Thus Far the Lord Has Helped Us

1. When trials begin and doubt creeps in,
when joy is turned to sorrow,
then come what may, we'll stand and say,
"We shall not fear tomorrow!"
We'll rest assured and trust the Lord,
for safe he's always kept us.
The proof is cast in our own past:
Thus far the Lord has helped us!

2. As Samuel, God's praise to tell,
the Stone of Help erected,
we'll raise our cry to testify:
"See how we've been protected!"
Though some who hear resent or sneer
at blessings God has dealt us,
this truth can't hide or be denied:
Thus far the Lord has helped us!

3. We can't explain why mortal pain
God's son endured to save us.
A wayward child now reconciled,
we marvel, "He forgave us!"
This gracious love from God above,
all undeserved, indwelt us.
Of wondrous things our spirit sings:
"Thus far the Lord has helped us!"

Themes/occasions: God's provision. God's power and protection. Salvation.
God's faithfulness. Adversity. Remembrance. Christian witness. Samuel.
God's love.

Scripture suggestions: 1 Samuel 7:10–12. Psalm 3:1–6. Psalm 22.
Psalm 46:1–7. Habakkuk 3:17–19.

Musical setting: CONSTANCE

98. When the Nothing I Am Meets the Great I Am

1. On the day that I die,
there'll be no alibi
when the soul-searching eyes of the Judge
see the evil I've done,
good deeds never begun.
I have failed him so often, so much! *R.*

R. No defense can I make
for my salvation's sake
when the nothing I am meets the Great I Am,
but to call out my claim
on the Son's holy name,
when the nothing I am meets the Great I Am.

2. If I ever believed
that he might be deceived,
I was fooling no one but myself,
for the Judge surely heard
every cruel and false word.
Every blow I have struck, he has felt. *R.*

3. But I won't be alone
when I kneel at the throne.
The Lord Jesus will take up my cause.
He will enter a plea
lifting all guilt from me,
for he ransomed my soul on the cross. *R.*

4. So I'll hope at the end
that I won't be condemned.
Undeserving, I may yet be spared.
And in spite of my sin
God will welcome me in,
to the heavenly home he's prepared. *R.*

Themes/occasions: Judgment. Redemption. Heaven. Eternal life. Salvation.

Scripture suggestions: Exodus 3:14. John 3:16–17. John 14:1–2. Acts 2:21.
Hebrews 4:12–16. 1 John 2:1–2. Ephesians 1:7. Ephesians 2:1–5.
2 Corinthians 5:17–19. Matthew 11:28–30. Romans 3:23–25. Romans 8:1–2.
Romans 6:20–23. Romans 10:13–15. Jude 1:24–25. Psalm 32:1–5.

Musical setting: THE NOTHING I AM

99. Where Are You, My Lord

1. Where are you, my Lord? How I need you today!
Oh, touch me, this very hour!
Your presence means more than the greatest display
of majesty and of power. *R.*

R. I miss you so, when you don't feel near!
Where did it go, your voice in my ear?
Lord, help me know you truly are here,
and stay, come what may, tomorrow.

2. Where are you, my Lord? How I want you to say,
"I'm with you, this very minute!"
I search your creation by night and by day,
but don't see your dear face in it. *R.*

3. Where are you, my Lord? Do you still hear me pray?
Please answer, this very second!
I wonder, are you simply too far away,
more busy than I had reckoned? *R.*

Themes/occasions: God's presence. Questioning. Prayer.
Scripture suggestions: Psalm 22. Psalm 88:13–14. Song of Solomon 3:2.
Song of Solomon 5:6. Romans 1:20.
Musical setting: LIGHT OF THE WORLD, alt.

100. Why, My God

R. Why, my God, have you forsaken me?
I call you night and day.
Why are you so far from helping me?
Don't stay so far away!

1. I plead from dawn to sunset and groan the whole night through,
"Lord, hurry to my rescue!" No answer comes from you. *R.*

2. You've always saved your people and listened to their cry.
Now, hear me in my trouble! Without your help, I'll die. *R.*

3. My enemies surround me. I have no place to hide.
They roar like hungry lions. Their jaws are open wide. *R.*

4. They mock me when I tell them, "My God, so wise and strong,
will soon be here to save me!" Lord, come! And prove them wrong! *R.*

5. Then I will sing your praises: "The Lord God saves his own!"
The world will know your glory and bow before your throne! *R.*

Themes/occasions: God's presence. God's power and protection. Prayer.
Adversity. Psalm songs. Social conflict. God's faithfulness. Questioning.
Scripture suggestions: Psalm 22. Matthew 27:46–50. Mark 15:33–39.
Musical setting: BALM IN GILEAD

101, 110.   Seventy Times Seven

1. Tell us, Jesus, how to treat
debtors who cannot repay.
You sit on the judgment seat.
Righteous One, what do you say?
Limitless in mercy, you
canceled our sin's heavy debt.
Your command is that we too
shall forgive and then forget.

2. You say vengeance is the Lord's;
bless, don't curse, our enemy.
Grace can cut these hateful cords,
and forgiving set us free.
Help us turn the other cheek,
mindful that we too have flaws.
Gentle justice we must seek,
and with love uphold your laws.

3. Lord, how many times must we
pardon those who do us wrong?
Seven times? Do you agree?
How we've suffered, for so long!
Seventy times seven, Lord!
Thus you bid us to forgive.
Then we'll reap this great reward:
In your peace our hearts will live.

Themes/occasions: Forgiveness. Love for neighbor. Justice. Judgment. Grace.
God's commands. Peace.

Scripture suggestions: 1 John 2:1–2. Matthew 5:23–24. Matthew 6:9–15.
Matthew 18:21–22. Luke 17:3–4. Romans 2:1–16. Colossians 3:12–13.
Ephesians 4:25–32. John 8:1–11.

Musical setting: MARTYN (#101); Now, O Now, I Needs Must Part (#110)

102, 103. Your Laws, O God

1. *(Psalmist)* Blessed are those who follow God's decrees,
those who strive the Lord alone to please.
In your rules, Lord, I (we) take delight.
I (We) will always try to do what's right.
Help me (us) live by your laws, O God.

2. *(Scoffers)* How can you sing such a happy song
when God's telling you what's right and wrong?
I'd (We'd) be singing the low-down blues
if my (our) pleasures I (we) were forced to lose.
Just ignore all the laws of God!

3. *(Psalmist)* Walking with my (our) God the whole day long,
I (we) can't help but sing a joyful song!
Grace and love chased away my (our) blues.
Life eternal, gratefully, I (we) choose.
Thanks and praise for your laws, O God!

4. *(Scoffers)* Bowing down to all of God's commands?
Why you want to, no one understands.
You will never succeed that way.
Only fools would willingly obey.
Let's forget all the laws of God!

5. *(Psalmist)* Keeping up with all the world's demands
looks so foolish next to God's good plans!
I (we) don't care what the scoffers say;
from your path I (we) never want to stray.
I (We) will live by your laws, O God!

Verses 2 and 4 are omitted from version #102.

Themes/occasions: God's commands. Obedience. Social conflict. God's plan.
Psalm songs. Temptation.
Scripture suggestions: Psalm 19:7–11. Psalm 119. 1 John 4:4–6. Jude 1:17–21.
Musical setting: HENDON

104. Oh, How You Have Loved Me, Jesus

1. Oh, how you have loved me, Jesus!
Love past understanding!
I have never known a love
so kind and undemanding.
Your life you give,
that I may live
with you forever and evermore.
No other love could be more true!
Oh, Jesus, how I love you!

2. You do not condemn me, Jesus!
Your smile reassures me.
For the many times I've sinned
your tender heart shows mercy.
You set me free.
Now I shall be
at peace forever and evermore.
No other love could be more true!
Oh, Jesus, how I love you!

Themes/occasions: God's love. Salvation. Redemption. Forgiveness. Love.
Eternal life. God's presence.

Scripture suggestions: 1 John 4:7–21. Psalm 138. Romans 5:6–11. Romans 6.
Jeremiah 31:3. Ephesians 3:14–21. Ephesians 4:31–32. John 3:16–18.
John 13:34–35. John 14. Philippians 4:7–8.

Musical setting: HYFRYDOL, alt.

105. Oh, How You Love Me, Jesus

Oh, how you love me, Jesus!
Love beyond understanding!
I've never known a love so
patient and undemanding.
You came not to condemn me,
your gracious smile assures me.
For all the times I've fallen
your tender heart shows mercy.
Your life you give,
that I may live
forever and evermore.
No love could be more true!
Jesus, how I love you!

Themes/occasions: God's love. Salvation. Redemption. Forgiveness. Love.
Eternal life. God's presence.
Scripture suggestions: 1 John 4:7–21. Psalm 138. Romans 5:6–11. Romans 6.
Jeremiah 31:3. Ephesians 3:14–21. Ephesians 4:31–32. John 3:16–18.
John 13:34–35. John 14. Philippians 4:7–8.
Musical setting: O Mio Babbino Caro

106. Let's Walk Each Other Home

1. Let's walk each other home,
where our friends and family wait.
Let's walk each other home,
hand in hand, to heaven's gate.
The road is dark and dreary,
but we will find our way;
the journey long and weary,
but we'll get home someday.

2. Alone, I can be vanquished
by sorrows, doubts, and fears.
Together, darkness banished,
we dry each other's tears.
We'll marvel at the blessing
life held for you and me,
our joyful hope professing:
The best, we've yet to see!

3. Perhaps the risen Jesus,
who perfect friendship showed,
will walk with us and teach us
on our Emmaus road.
Let's walk each other home,
where our friends and family wait.
Let's walk each other home,
all the way to heaven's gate.

Themes/occasions: Unity. Love for neighbor. God's presence. Heaven.
Death and dying. Community of faith.

Scripture suggestions: Luke 24:13–31. John 15:9–17. Ephesians 3:14–21.
Ecclesiastes 4:9–12.

Musical setting: ST. CHRISTOPHER

This page is left blank in order to display the following songs on facing pages. Feel free to scribble notes here.

107. My God, Why

1. "My God, why?"
resounds on Calvary,
where now the man
called Jesus, King of the Jews,
hangs crucified.
"My God, my God, oh why
have you forsaken me?"
Not one command
did Jesus refuse.
Why now does the face of God hide?

2. One last cry,
exclaiming, "It is done!"
Triumphant words!
His spirit he will soon yield
to hands above.
Almighty God on high,
well pleased, awaits his Son.
Jesus endures
his final ordeal
in perfect, obedient love.

3. Dark noon sky.
Earth quakes. Creation knows!
The temple veil
from top to bottom is torn
as Jesus dies.
When soldiers pierce his side,
blood mixed with water flows.
Onlookers wail
and followers mourn
when cold in a tomb Jesus lies.

4. Tear-swelled eyes
in dawning light behold
an empty grave!
Rejoice! He once again lives
who had been slain!
Death's pow'r the Christ defies.
He keeps God's word of old,
sinners to save.
New life Jesus gives,
in glory forever to reign!

Themes/occasions: Calvary. Good Friday. Easter. Holy Week. God's presence. The cross. Jesus Christ's ministry and miracles. Salvation. God's promises. Obedience.

Scripture suggestions: Psalm 22:1. Matthew 27:45–50. Mark 15:33–39. Romans 5:6–11. 1 John 2:1–2. 1 John 4:9–18. Philippians 2:5–8.

Musical setting: Time Stands Still

108. Love the Lord (SATB)

1. Love the Lord, the God of Abraham!
To prosper in the land,
full love is his command:
your heart, your mind, your soul, your might,
* with all that you possess!
The Lord demands no less.

*(A/B) with everything that you possess!
(T) with everything that you possess. Yes, everything!

2. Love the Lord, and love your fellow man
as truly as you can.
This, too, is God's command.
Be just, be kind, be meek, do right
* to all, both rich and poor.
The Lord demands no more.

*(A/B) to everyone, both rich and poor.
(T) to everyone, both rich and poor. Yes, everyone!

3. Love the Lord: Lord Jesus, Son of Man,
Son of the Great I Am,
the pure and holy Lamb,
the Bread, the Vine, the Way, the Light,
* of all the highest name,
from age to age the same.

*(A/B) of every name the highest name,
(T) of every name the highest name. Yes, every name!

Themes/occasions: Love for God. Love for neighbor. God's commands.
Scripture suggestions: Deuteronomy 6:4–9. Mark 12:28–31. Romans 1:1–6.
Revelation 5. Micah 6:8. James 2:1–5. Philippians 2:8–11. Exodus 3:14.
John 1:29–31. John 6:25–59. John 14:1–7. John 8:12. John 15:1–17.
Musical setting: Come Again

109. Unchain My Soul (SATB)

1. Unchain my soul and set me free,
free from the sin that shackles me,
to soar (oh so) high by your side.
Fill me with grace (I pray) and make me new,
a fresh creation, Lord, a pure and pleasing one to you,
by your blood sanctified.

2. Comfort my heart; relieve my care.
Lift from my back the weight I bear,
and mute this (noisy) world's demands.
Bind up my wounds, (I pray,) that I may heal.
Upon my body, Lord, pour out your balm and let me feel
the sweet touch of your hands.

3. Speak to me, Lord. Indwell my mind.
No wiser master could I find
to teach (me) truth from (God) above.
You know my name (so well). Oh, call me near,
to listen at your feet, the better all your words to hear,
words of mercy and love.

4. Strengthen my hand that I may fight
your righteous cause with holy might,
your flag (bravely) flying unfurled.
Quicken my steps, (O Lord,) that I with haste
may take the welcome news of your redeeming love and grace
to the whole waiting world!

Themes/occasions: Freedom. Grace. Renewal. Spiritual warfare. Truth.
Comfort. Healing. Sin. Discipleship. Salvation. Evangelism.
Scripture suggestions: 1 John 5:1–5. Romans 6:20–23. Romans 8:1–2.
Romans 10:13–15. Romans 12:1–2. Isaiah 41:10–13. Galatians 5:1.
2 Corinthians 5:17. Luke 10:38–42. Matthew 11:28–30.
Musical setting: Awake, Sweet Love

110. Seventy Times Seven

See #101

111.   The One That Was Lost

1. A shepherd noticed that one lamb was missing.
A sheep is in danger who wanders alone.
And the shepherd so loved his wee frightened lamb
that he hurried to find it and bring it back home.
I'm the one that was lost, O my Lord, my Shepherd,
the one from your sheepfold who foolishly strayed.
I'm the lamb you cared for enough to keep searching,
yes, leaving behind ninety-nine who obeyed.

2. A humble woman saved ten coins of silver,
but one day a coin fell and rolled on the ground.
So she lit a lamp and swept out every corner
and called all her friends when her lost coin was found.
I'm the one that was lost, O my Lord, my Savior,
the small piece of silver that fell to the floor.
I'm the coin you valued enough to keep sweeping.
All heaven rejoiced when you held me once more.

3. A father granted his younger son's wishes
to spend his inheritance now, as he pleased.
But he watched, and when his son came home in tatters
he ran to embrace him and called for a feast.
I'm the one that was lost, O my Lord, my Father,
the sinner who squandered your hard-earned estate.
I'm the child you cherished enough to keep watching.
You ran out to meet me and cried, "Celebrate!"

Themes/occasions: Good Shepherd. Father God. Father's Day. God's love.
God's faithfulness. Forgiveness. God's power and protection.
Scripture suggestions: Luke 15:3–7. Luke 15:8–10. Luke 15:11–24.
Matthew 18:12–13.
Musical setting: CANDLER/YE BANKS AND BRAES

112. Only Then

1. A storm of hatred rages,
    close to home and far abroad.
Sharp as cracks of thunder,
    the angry shouts come crashing on my ear.
I press my hands against my head
and yearn for just one gentle word instead.

Only then do I begin to hear
the still, small voice of God.

2. I strain to see the truth
    behind the dazzling glare of fraud.
Bright as bursts of lightning,
    false promises and pride are blinding me.
I pull the shutters toward my heart
and slowly grow accustomed to the dark.

Only then do I begin to see
the faint, pure light of God.

3. A rising tide of loneliness
    floods every waking thought.
Oh, so many sorrows!
    My spirit drowns in pain that will not heal.
I struggle to a higher place
and let the chill air dry my upturned face.

Only then do I begin to feel
the tender tears of God.

4. A hurricane of changes
    throws me off the path I trod.
Chaos looms before me,
    the wreckage of my dreams lies strewn behind.
I seek a shelter from the wind,
a calm to get my bearings once again.

Only then do I begin to find
my way back home to God:
to the voice, the light, the peace,
    the all-transcending love of God.

Themes/occasions: God's presence. Light. Social conflict. Temptation. Truth. Mourning. Peace. Mental illness. Guidance. God's love. Seeker. Hope. Adversity. Comfort. Loss. Renewal. Prayer. Rest. Love.

Scripture suggestions: 1 Kings 19:11–13. Romans 8:26–27. Romans 8:38–39. Romans 12:2. Psalm 46:10–11. Psalm 91:1–5. Philippians 4:7–8. Matthew 6:6–8. 1 Chronicles 16:11. Luke 5:15–16. Mark 1:35–37. Zephaniah 3:17. Lamentations 3:25–28.

Musical setting: ONLY THEN, alt.

113. How I Love to Use My Hands

1. How I love to use my hands
and labor all day long
to fulfill the holy plans
for which you made me strong!
If tomorrow, Lord, you take
my pow'r to toil away,
I still will give you praise
for giving me my working days.

2. How I love to use my feet
and legs so swift and strong!
On the highway, trail, and street,
I bring your Word along.
If tomorrow, Lord, you take
my pow'r to walk away,
I still will give you praise
for giving me my running days.

3. How I love to use my voice
to sing your Gospel song,
telling sinners to rejoice,
in tones so sweet and strong!
If tomorrow, Lord, you take
my pow'r to speak away,
I still will give you praise
for giving me my singing days.

4. How I love to use my mind,
my mem'ry clear and strong,
to explore your grand design
and learn what's right and wrong!
If tomorrow, Lord, you take
my pow'r of thought away,
I still will give you praise
for giving me my thinking days.

5. How I love to simply be,
no matter weak or strong!
Thank you for creating me!
To you I do belong.
If tomorrow, Lord, you take
my very life away,
I still will give you praise
for giving me my earthly days.

Themes/occasions: Praise. Sovereign Lord. Thanksgiving. Creation. Loss.
Adversity. Death and dying. Music.

Scripture suggestions: 1 Thessalonians 5:16–18. Job 1. Daniel 3. Psalm 61.
Ephesians 5:18–20. Ecclesiastes 3:9–13. Isaiah 52:7.

Musical setting: BLAIRGOWRIE, alt.

114.   Whom Shall We Fear

1. Whom shall we fear, if God is on our side?
No charge can stand against those justified
through faith in Christ, who for our pardon died.
Alleluia! Alleluia!

2. What tribulation, danger, depths, or heights
shall part us from God's love in Jesus Christ?
No pow'r in all creation could suffice!
Alleluia! Alleluia!

3. When shall we be abandoned and alone,
if God adopts us as his very own?
We're heirs with Christ, not orphaned, not unknown.
Alleluia! Alleluia!

4. Where shall defense for disbelief be found,
with proof of God's true nature all around?
There's no excuse; in Christ, clear signs abound.
Alleluia! Alleluia!

5. How shall we say that we're not rich enough,
if wealth is weighed by Christ's abundant love?
No thief can steal our treasures stored above.
Alleluia! Alleluia!

6. Why shall we mourn the end of mortal days,
if we believe God's faithful shall be raised?
Weep not, but sing! Let Jesus Christ be praised!
Alleluia! Alleluia!

Themes/occasions: Faith. God's provision. God's power and protection.
Eternal life. Salvation. Social conflict. Heaven. Adversity. Death and dying.
Scripture suggestions: Romans 1:19–20. Romans 8:14–39. Psalm 3:1–6.
Psalm 27:1–6. Matthew 6:19–21. Philippians 1:21–24. Ephesians 3:14–21.
1 Thessalonians 4:13–14.
Musical settings: SINE NOMINE; SARUM

115. Faith Isn't Just a State of Mind

1. Faith isn't just a state of mind
where unbelief is left behind.
Each day we hear a still, small voice:
Faith calling us to make a choice.

2. Faith overcomes the fiercest doubt
but dies unless we act it out.
Come, keep alive our faith in Christ,
through deeds of love and sacrifice.

Themes/occasions: Faith. Service.
Scripture suggestions: James 2:14–26. Hebrews 11. Luke 18:18–23.
Matthew 19:16–22. Mark 10:17–27.
Musical setting: OLD 100th

116. Side by Side

1. Side by side, hand in hand,
walk with me to the Promised Land.

2. When you hurt, I will care.
Kneel with me, and we'll say a prayer.

3. We'll find hope if we look.
Read with me from the Holy Book.

4. With God's help, we are strong.
Sing with me a triumphant song.

Themes/occasions: Unity. Love for neighbor. God's power and protection.
Death and dying. Hope. Heaven. Community of faith. The Bible. Prayer.
Healing.

Scripture suggestions: Ecclesiastes 4:9–12. Jeremiah 29:10–14. John 15:9–17.
Romans 12:9–18. Acts 2:41–47. 2 Timothy 3:14–17.

Musical setting: SIDE BY SIDE (Round)

117. Soon Sets the Sun

1. Soon sets the sun.
I've done all I can do.
Now, Holy One,
I give it all to you.
Use, if you will,
my words and deeds, though flawed.
I will be still
and know that you are God.

2. Nighttime is nigh.
Your spirit speaks to me
soft as a sigh.
"Let go, and let it be."
Grant, if you will,
your peace so deep and broad.
I will be still
and know that you are God.

Themes/occasions: Peace. Evening. Rest. Prayer. God's presence. Comfort.
Social conflict. Service. Hope. Trust. Death and dying. Sovereign Lord.
Funerals and memorials. God's provision.

Scripture suggestions: 1 Kings 19:11–13. Romans 8:26–27. Psalm 46:10–11.
Psalm 91:1–5. Philippians 4:7–8. Matthew 6:6–8. Matthew 6:25–34.
Matthew 11:28–30. Mark 1:35–37. 1 Chronicles 16:11. Zephaniah 3:17.
Lamentations 3:25–28.

Musical setting: EVENTIDE

Indexes

INDEX OF SCRIPTURE

INDEX OF THEMES AND OCCASIONS

INDEX OF TITLES AND FIRST LINES

ACKNOWLEDGMENTS

The release of *Now Sings My Soul: New Songs for the Lord* marks the ten-year anniversary of my covenant with the Lord to write according to his daily direction. Collaborating with my Holy GhostWriter has been a joyful, demanding, and fruitful experience. None of these songs, or any of my other writings, would have been conceived, let alone delivered, without that creative partnership.

Bill Olin, my husband of forty-plus years, is in a one-man category of people to thank. Bill is more into cows and tractors than poetry and "Holy GhostWriter" talk, but he's still my biggest cheerleader.

I'm deeply grateful for all the kindred spirits who have encouraged, supported, and prayed for my songwriting and publishing efforts. Chief among them are Lida Bassler; Rev. Emrys Tyler; Pattie Lengel; the late Roger Goodwin; my writing cronies in Afton, Walton, Montrose, and Facebook groups; and above all my dear "Ma," the late Theresa Bonney.

Special thanks to the following:

- Pastor Sue Crawson-Brizzolara, whose sermons have supplied fodder for many a hymn text
- Phyllis Neff Lake and Theresa Olin for lending their expertise to the development of accompaniments for my original melodies
- Theresa Olin and Tony Villecco for gracing my YouTube channel with their exquisite vocals
- The music ministers and hymn-lovers who have test-driven and critiqued my new pieces, especially the pastors, musicians, and congregations of Harpursville United Methodist Church, Minot United Methodist Church, Nineveh Presbyterian Church, and West Minot Union Church
- Lauren Floden, whose inspired harp helped start me on the road to writing music

- Hymnary.org, The Cyber Hymnal™ (hymntime.com/tch), NetHymnal (cyberhymnal.org), and SmallChurchMusic.com for supplying digital scores of public domain tunes
- The MuseScore developers and community for their commitment to free, open source music notation software (musescore.org and musescore.com)
- The posse of Bible readers who recommended scripture references for this book, especially Lisa Kesinger DeVinney, Ann Marin Frizzell, Vi Gommer, and Angela Davis

Last but not least, I salute the composers and arrangers who have gone to their eternal rewards, leaving behind inspiring tunes that give wings to my words. May their work gain fresh appreciation as these songs are sung.

ABOUT THE AUTHOR

Linda Bonney Olin, a graduate of Cornell University and member of the Hymn Society in the United States and Canada, was certified as a lay speaker in the United Methodist Church in 1997. Her poems, devotions, short fiction, hymns, and Bible study materials have been published in anthologies, literary and devotional magazines, and online publications. She has served on faculty at Montrose Christian Writers Conference and has developed and presented devotional programs for multi-denominational church groups, often featuring original drama and/or music.

Visit the Faith Songs website (LindaBonneyOlin.com) to learn more about Linda Bonney Olin, contact her, and find a variety of resources for ministry, music, and writing. Check the Audio page for samples of the music from this book and other projects. Hear recordings of vocal performances of selected hymns and faith songs on YouTube (youtube.com/LindaBonneyOlin).

Previously published texts that appear in *Now Sings My Soul: New Songs for the Lord:*

- My Forever Lord (Utmost Christian Writers Poetry Gallery, Christian Publishers Poetry Prize: 2nd place rhymed poem, 2010; *Songs for the Lord*, 2012; *The Lord Our Wonderful Healer*, 2013)

- A Lamb in the Wilderness (*The War Cry*, 2014; selected for performance at United Theological Seminary's New Songs and Hymns for Renewal concert, 2012)

- Jesus Walks on City Streets (*Worship in the City*, United Church of Canada, 2015)

- Family Circle of God (*The War Cry*, 2016; *Songs for the Lord*, 2012; *The Secret Place*, 2011)

- Because You Loved Me First (*Penned from the Heart*, 2013)

- Roll the Stone Away; Where Were the Twelve; My God, Why; Jesus, Please Remember Me; Where Are You, My God (*Were You There When They Crucified Our Lord*, 2017)

- Oh, How You Love Me Jesus (*Transformed: 5 Resurrection Dramas*, 2014)

- Before Us, Alive; Don't Be Afraid; In the Armor of God; Maybe Yes and Maybe No; My Footprints on Your Life; Only Then; People of God Keep Grumbling; The Uphill Road; Thy Will Be Done; When the Nothing I Am Meets the Great I Am; You Didn't Just Give Us Light (*Songs for the Lord*, 2012)

MORE BOOKS BY LINDA BONNEY OLIN

Were You There When They Crucified Our Lord?
Meditations on Calvary

Calvary through the eyes of those present when Jesus Christ was arrested and crucified, including:
- the Roman and religious authorities;
- the twelve;
- the women;
- the jeering onlookers.

Six chapters of scripture readings, meditations, songs, discussion questions, and prayers.

Transformed:
5 Resurrection Dramas

Five one-act plays to read or perform with a small cast. Each play explores how a person close to Jesus was transformed by his resurrection:
- Simon Peter (dramatic comedy)
- John the Apostle (dramatic monologue)
- James the Brother of Jesus (dramatic comedy with five short ensemble songs; plus an alternate interview version)
- Mary the Mother of Jesus (light drama)
- Mary Magdalene (dramatic monologue with optional solo songs)

Songs for the Lord:
A Book of Twenty-Four Original Hymns and Faith Songs

Linda Bonney Olin's first book of songs. A mix of traditional and contemporary styles, from soulful solos to hand-clapping gospel to humorous troubadour-style songs. Original lyrics and melodies; no piano accompaniment.

The Sacrifice Support Group:
A Dramatic Comedy for Lent

A mixed bag of church characters are challenged by their pastor to make Lenten sacrifices that glorify God and benefit their families and community—even the world!

Two twenty-minute acts. Cast: 1 M, 3 F; 3 M/F. Ideal for actors with limited mobility. Virtually no staging required. Easy to put on as Readers Theatre with little or no preparation.

Giving It Up for Lent:
Bible Study, Drama, Discussion

A fun, challenging, and possibly life-changing study on the tradition of Lenten sacrifices, featuring *The Sacrifice Support Group*. Includes an introductory look at Bible accounts of people who offered sacrifices (some pleasing to the Lord, others not), in-depth discussion questions, and the drama script. For adults and older teens.

www.ingramcontent.com/pod-product-compliance
Lightning Source LLC
Chambersburg PA
CBHW051826040426
42447CB00006B/391